Aesop's Fables
(a selection)

An Intermediate
Ancient Greek Reader

C. T. Hadavas

Aesop's Fables (A Selection)
An Intermediate Ancient Greek Reader
Ancient Greek text with vocabulary and commentary

First Edition

© 2016 by C. T. Hadavas

The Greek texts are those of Émile Chambry, Ben E. Perry, and Francesco Sbordone

ISBN-13: 978-1536830484
ISBN-10: 1536830488

Published by C. T. Hadavas

Cover Design: C. T. Hadavas

Cover Image: Cover art by C. T. Hadavas, based off of Arthur Rackham's illustration for the fable of the Fox and the Grapes from the first page of *Aesop's Fables: A New Translation by V. S. Vernon Jones, with an Introduction by G. K. Chesterton, and Illustrations by Arthur Rackham* (London, 1912)

Credits:

Hill's translations of La Fontaine are from:
Craig Hill, *The Complete Fables of La Fontaine* (New York: Arcade Publishing, 2008) and are reprinted by permission of Skyhorse Publishing, Inc.

All images appearing in this edition are in the public domain, with the exception of those by Jacob Lawrence, which are copyright-protected and appear in this edition by permission of The Jacob and Gwendolyn Knight Lawrence Foundation, Seattle / Artists Rights Society (ARS), New York

Fonts: (English) Times New Roman; (Greek) GFS Porson

German woodcut, frontispiece from *Aesop's Life and Fables* (Ulm; c. 1476-77)

Aesop as a hunchback (part of his apocryphal biographical tradition), surrounded by a seemingly random assemblage of images allusively (and rather cryptically) referencing certain of his fables.

TABLE OF CONTENTS

ACKNOWLEDGMENTS

In the field of Aesopic studies there are three individuals whose work has been of particular importance to me:

- Ben E. Perry, professor of classics at the University of Illinois at Urbana-Champaign from 1924 to 1960, whose pioneering research on Aesop's fables and on ancient popular literature in general has helped redefine what the study of classical literature can be

- Laura Gibbs, whose advocacy for and popularization of Aesop in print (*Aesop's Fables*, *Aesop's Fables in Latin: Ancient Wit and Wisdom from the Animal Kingdom*) and on the web (www.mythfolklore.net/aesopica) beautifully complement Perry's more traditional scholarship

- Reverend Gregory I. Carlson, S.J., whose assiduously assembled and annotated collection of Aesopic printed books and miscellanea (https://www.creighton.edu/aesop/books/) evinces an incredible passion for the fables and their journeys through time

C. T. Hadavas
Chair, Department of Classics, Beloit College
(October 2016)

viii

How To Use This Book

This book is designed for students who, at a minimum, are finishing, or who have just finished, the first year of college Ancient Greek. It is also for individuals who studied Ancient Greek years ago and would like to return to the language and its literature in as easy and engaging a manner as possible.

The reader for *Aesop's Fables (a selection)* is assumed to have a basic acquaintance with Ancient Greek grammar. All vocabulary found in the fable on the left page, with the exception of the verb $\epsilon\dot{\iota}\mu\dot{\iota}$, personal pronouns, and the most common conjunctions (e.g., $\dot{\alpha}\lambda\lambda\dot{\alpha}$, $\kappa\alpha\dot{\iota}$), adverbs (e.g., $o\dot{\upsilon}$, $\mu\dot{\eta}$), and particles (e.g., $\mu\dot{\epsilon}\nu$, $\delta\dot{\epsilon}$), is given either below the text or on the facing page. For many verbs only the first person singular present active indicative form is provided. For verbs with unusual forms (e.g., those with deponent futures, second aorists, or with futures and aorists from unrelated stems) the first person singular active forms of the present, future, and aorist are, where warranted, given. For -$\mu\iota$ verbs the second aorist active and/or the perfect active, where warranted, are also provided.

On the understanding that readers of this book have either just finished the first year of college Ancient Greek, or are returning after a hiatus of some time from their study of the language, rather detailed grammatical and syntactical notes have been provided.

A special feature of this text is the generous selection of different versions of the fables that have been created over time. Although several of these are translations of La Fontaine's celebrated French versions, the majority are from the rich tradition of English translations/adaptations made since the publication of William Caxton's first English Aesop in 1484. Many of these English texts (some derived from Greek versions – not necessarily the ones printed in this text –, others from Latin versions) have themselves become part of the fable tradition.

Finally, I have also included a substantial number of illustrations from the 18th to the 20th centuries that showcase various approaches – simple representation, humorous spin, contemporary social commentary, etc. – that artists have employed in illuminating the fables. Indeed, as John McKendry notes in the introduction to *Aesop: Five Centuries of Illustrated Fables* (Greenwich, Connecticut: Metropolitan Museum of Art, 1964, 5), "The fables of Aesop are the only text that has been illustrated so often, so diversely, and so continuously that the history of the printed illustrated book can be shown by them alone."

INTRODUCTION

"Aesop embodies an epigram not uncommon in human history; his fame is all the more deserved because he never deserved it. The firm foundations of common sense, the shrewd shots at uncommon sense, that characterise all the Fables, belong not to him but to humanity. In the earliest human history whatever is authentic is universal: and whatever is universal is anonymous. In such cases there is always some central man who had first the trouble of collecting them, and afterwards the fame of creating them. He had the fame; and, on the whole, he earned the fame. There must have been something great and human, something of the human future and the human past, in such a man: even if he only used it to rob the past or deceive the future."

(G. K. Chesterton, from his Introduction to *Aesop's Fables:*
A New Translation by V. S. Vernon Jones. London, 1912)

I. Aesop and his Fables

The fables now inextricably linked to the name of Aesop were first passed down orally over many centuries in the languages of the various peoples of the Eastern Mediterranean and Ancient Near East. Sometime between the fifth and fourth centuries BCE, many of the Greek versions of these short tales were said to have been skillfully told by a master storyteller who supposedly was alive at the beginning of the 6th century BCE.[1] This legendary figure, to whom the name Aesop was attached by the Greeks, is a shadowy figure about whom next to nothing is known.[2]

As far as one can tell, the Greek fables were first collected together at the end of the fourth century BCE by the scholar Demetrius of Phalerum (c. 350 – c. 280). Later fable writers in Greek and Latin left their own stamp on the tradition, many of them anonymously. The vast majority of these latter-day Aesops lived during the period from c. 100 BCE to c. 400 CE, though a few (e.g., Odo of Cheriton) were writing in the Middle Ages. The Greek fables were, for the most part, written in what we now call Koine Greek ($\dot{\eta}$ κοινὴ διάλεκτος, 'the common dialect [sc. of Greek]'), the language of spoken discourse and of much written communication

---

[1] Aesop is first mentioned by the Greek historian Herodotus (2.134-5) as a sixth-century BCE slave of a certain Iadmon, a citizen of the island of Samos.

[2] Later Greeks, curious about the story of Aesop's life, created a fictional account that often appears together with the fables in the Byzantine manuscript tradition. This so-called *Life of Aesop* is an eclectic and engaging set of narrative episodes best read in Lloyd Daly's translation (available both in Daly and in W. Hansen's *Anthology of Ancient Greek Popular Literature* [Bloomington, IN: Indiana University Press, 1998]).

employed by Greek speakers in the eastern half of the Roman empire from the Hellenistic period to the beginning of the Middle Ages.

Aesopic fables that exist today – even ones that appear quite simple in their narrative – are *literary* retellings built upon earlier (and invariably oral) fokloric scaffoldings. The fables themselves, though, even if temporarily pinned down by written words, remain polymorphous, and thus open to reinterpretation and revision by later storytellers. There is no longer (if there ever, in fact, was) an 'original' Aesopic fable: there exist only collections of possible variations.[3] Sometimes, as in the case of Babrius, a Hellenized Roman writing in the late 1st century CE, the fable aspires to a certain poetic sophistication. At other times, however, it appears disguised in the garb of an oral folk tale – 'simple' only in facile comparison with its more overtly literary brethren. Both versions are equally 'Aesopic,' as are, for example, the elaborate renditions of the 17th-century Roger L'Estrange (twelve of which are included in this book) and the terse limericks of the late 19th-century W. J. Linton (seven of which are included in this book – one of which also adorns the back cover where it appears in its original setting accompanying Walter Crane's illustration).

II. Not for Children

Lloyd Daly, who has written the most genial (and perhaps best) introduction to Aesop's fables, notes that:

"When the Greek looked at himself, he was not always happy with what he saw.... The Aesopic fables are one of these reflections from the mirror of self-examination. The Greek looks into his glass and sees a horrible picture of himself. It is always difficult to be honest with oneself, and it is as though the fables were saying, "It is not I but the animal in me that is like this." Then comes the moralist and says, "No, you fool; this is yourself even more truly than any ideal you may have." The Aesopic fables have been pap for children in schools for so many hundreds of years that is is perhaps difficult to think of them in any other light, but the cynical vein of the stories themselves runs so strong that that it must be obvious they were not intended for the edification of youth,..."[4]

Indeed, in the ancient world, the fables were deployed by a variety of adults (e.g., comic playwrights, philosophers) for other adults. Although Aesopic

---

[3] Cf. Perry 1936, 73: "a definitive edition of the *Fables* never existed, at least none that was universally recognized as such and as coming from the pen of Aesop himself."

[4] Daly, 11-12.

fables have a range of uses (e.g., aetiological, satirical, moral – this last being, in fact, quite rare until later periods), "the vast majority are paradigmatic, which is to say that, whatever their content, they serve as examples, usually horrible, of human behavior."[5]

III. Parts of the Fable

Depending on the writer and the tradition, an Aesopic fable (usually) can have up to three distinct parts (though the second as listed below is by far the most common).

The first possible part that one might encounter in terms of the spatial-chronological sequence of the narration is the **promythium**, a moral that comes *before* (πρό) *the fable* (μῦθος), so that the reader/listener can properly decode the meaning of the narrative. In the selection of fables in this text, only Aphthonius's versions (3, 25) have this feature.

The second possible component is the **fable body with endomythium**. This is the essential core of all fables. In fact, many fables have nothing but this part (though Aphthonius' fables, for the most part, lack this element). The **endomythium** is the moral *within* (ἔνδον) *the fable* (μῦθος), usually told by one of the actors in the story's narration.

The last possible part is the **epimythium**, a moral *added at the end* (ἐπί) *of the fable* (μῦθος) to make sure that the point of the story is clear. Many, though not all, fables have **epimythia**, though it is evident both from their linguistic usage and, occasionally, in terms of their contradicting the fable's **endomythium**, that the great majority of **epimythia** were composed by later copyists/writers, either to reinforce the message of the **endomythium** or to correct/redirect it.

---

[5] Daly, 17. The best discussion of a fable's definition is by Reverend Gregory I. Carlson, S.J., and can be found at: https://www.creighton.edu/aesop/intro/definition/)]

IV. Named Fable Authors Writing in Greek That Appear in This Text

Aphthonius (of Antioch): according to Gibbs (xxiii), "Aphthonius was a scholar and teacher of the fourth century CE associated with the school of Libanius. The fables of Aphthonius are forty in number.... In general, Aphthonius' fables are attested in other ancient sources, althrough there are a few fables which are otherwise unknown. As a rule, his fables are quite brief and, with few exceptions, he includes both a promythium and an epimythium for every fable. Given this abundance of editorial moralizing, it is not surprising that in the majority of Aphthonius' fables there is no endomythium, those witty last words spoken by one of the characters inside the fable itself."

Babrius, Valerius (?): according to Hopkinson (OCD³), "[Babrius,] probably from Syria or Asia Minor, composed not later than the 2nd cent. AD... Μυθίαμβοι Αἰσώπειοι, 'Fables of Aesop in Iambics', being versions in choliamic metre of existing fables, together perhaps with some additions or adaptations of his own. The work is more likely to have been originally in two books...than in ten...; 144 fables survive. The choliamb seems by this period to have lost its satirical overtones and to have been associated with chatty entertainment. Babrius' language is basically *koinē* Greek, but has an admixture of high poeticisms. The literary and artistic claims made in his two extant proems are such as to suggest that despite the apparent artlessness of his style, he wrote for the delectation of an educated public rather than for the schoolroom. His collection enjoyed great popularity, and was paraphrased in prose and verse in the Middle Ages."

Syntipas: as Gibbs (xxiv) notes, "The fables attributed to 'Syntipas' are actually the work of Michael Andreopulus, a [Byzantine] Greek scholar of the eleventh century [CE] who translated a collection of Syriac fables into Greek. Those Syriac fables, in turn, had originally been translated from Greek either in late antiquity or even well into the Middle Ages. There are slightly over sixty fables in this collection.... The significance of the Syntipas fables becomes clear when we realize that fifteen, approximately one quarter of the collection, are not attested elsewhere in the Aesopic corpus. Thanks to their preservation in Syriac, the fables of Syntipas escaped extinction, while we can only speculate about the hundreds or even thousands of other Greek fables that vanished along with their manuscripts (not to mention all the fables that were never even recorded in written form). Although the fables of Syntipas reach us by a roundabout path (from Greek to Syriac and back into Greek again), they remain quite lively. Most importantly, the fables of Syntipas regularly include an edomythium, the witty moral inside the story, in addition to the moralizing epimythium that concludes the tale."

THE CHOLIMAIC METER OF BABRIUS

Unlike the Greek prose texts in this book's selection of Aesopic fables, Babrius composed his versions in choliambic verse (Gk. χωλίαμβος, 'limping/lame iambic [verse]'). The basic structure of this meter is much like iambic trimeter (x – ˘ –), except that the last cretic (i.e., – ˘ –) is made heavy by the insertion of a long instead of a short (thus creating a dragging or 'limp' to the meter's rhythm). Also, the third anceps (i.e., a metrical syllable that can be either long or short, and noted in the scansion as an 'x') of the iambic trimeter line must be short in limping iambs. In other words, the line generally scans as follows:

$$x - \smile - \mid x - \smile - \mid \smile - - -$$

Below is the scansion for the first five lines of Babrius 64 (#14. The Fir Tree and the Bramble Bush, in this text):

```
  –  –  ˘  ˘ ˘ |–  –   ˘  – |  ˘   –  –  –
Ἥριζον ἐλάτη καὶ βάτος πρὸς ἀλλήλας.
 ˘  ˘  –   ˘  –  |–  –   ˘  – |˘  –  –  –
ἐλάτης δ' ἑαυτὴν πολλαχῶς ἐπαινούσης·
  –  –  ˘  –  |˘  –  –  ˘  – |  ˘  –  –  –
"καλὴ μέν εἰμι καὶ τὸ μέτρον εὐμήκης,
  –   –   ˘  – |–  –  ˘  – |˘– –  –
καὶ τῶν νεφῶν σύνοικος ὀρθίη φύω,
 ˘  –  –  ˘ ˘ |  ˘  –  ˘ ˘ – |  ˘  –    – –
στέγης τε μέλαθρον εἰμι καὶ τρόπις πλοίων
```

Note the substitution (technically called 'resolution') of two shorts for a long with ἐλάτη in the fourth foot of line 1 and the first foot (the anceps) of line 2, and with the first two syllables of the word μέλαθρον in line 5 (the second syllable of μέλαθρον, -αθρ-, can be either long or short since it has the combination of plosive [θ] + liquid [ρ]).

BIBLIOGRAPHIC ABBREVIATIONS

Daly   Daly, Lloyd. *Aesop Without Morals*. New York: Yoseloff, 1961

Gibbs   Gibbs, L. *Aesop's Fables*. Oxford: Oxford University Press, 2002

OCD³   Hornblower, S. and A. Spaworth, eds. *The Oxford Classical dictionary*. 3rd edn., Oxford, 1996

Perry 1936 Perry, B. E. *Studies in the Text History of the Life and Fables of Aesop*. Lancaster, Pennsylvania: American Philological Association, 1936

Perry 1952 Perry, Ben E. (ed.) *Aesopica*. Urbana, IL: University of Illinois Press, 1952

Perry 1965 Perry, Ben E. (ed.). *Babrius and Phaedrus*. Cambridge, Mass.: Harvard University Press, 1965

Smyth   Smyth, H. W. *Greek Grammar*, rev. G. M. Messing. Cambridge, Mass.: Harvard University Press, 1956

THE TEXTS

The texts used in this edition are from:

- Chambry, Aemilius (Émile). *Aesopi Fabulae*. Paris, 1925-1926: Fables 1, 2, 4, 5a + b, 6, 7, 9, 10, 11, 12, 13, 15, 17, 20, 21, 22, 23, 24, 27, 28, 31, 32, 34 || All references are to Chambry's first edition, which has numerous variants of each fable. If two numbers appear (e.g., 2 = Chambry 37/37), the second refers to Chambry's second edition (1927), which contains only a single version of each fable. Because of a slight change in numbering, the numbers in the second edition sometimes differ from those of the first edition

- Perry, Ben E. *Aesopica*. Urbana, IL, 1952: Fables 8, 18, 30

- Perry, Ben E. *Babrius and Phaedrus*. Cambridge, Mass., 1965: Fables 14, 16, 19, 26, 29, 33

- Sbordone, Francesco. "Recensioni retoriche delle favole esopiane," *Rivista Indo-Greco-Italica* 16 (1932), 47-57: Fables 3, 25

Daly, Lloyd. *Aesop Without Morals*. New York: Yoseloff, 1961

[In addition to a very large number of fables, Daly provides an English translation of the *Life of Aesop*, a fictional, episodic (but highly readable) late Hellenistic-early Empire novella/folkbook that follows Perry's critical edition. Illustrations by Grace Muscarella.]

Gibbs, Laura. *Aesop's Fables*. Oxford: Oxford University Press, 2002

[Includes 359 fables, with selections from all the major Greek and Latin sources, including those from the Middle Ages.]

Handford, S. A. *Fables of Aesop*. New York: Penguin, 1954

[Includes 207 fables, with illustrations by Brian Robb.]

Hull, Denison B. *Aesop's Fables: Told by Valerius Babrius*. Chicago: University of Chicago Press, 1960

[An engaging verse translation of Babrius's Aesopic poems that is also an excellent complement to Perry's prose renditions from his Loeb edition.]

Perry, Ben E. (ed.). *Babrius and Phaedrus*. Cambridge, MA: Harvard University Press, 1965

[An excellent duo-language version in the Loeb series, with Greek text and English prose translation (Babrius) as well as Latin text and English prose translation (Phaedrus). Also contains several helpful introductions, a lengthy appendix that provides an analytical survey of Greek and Latin fables in the Aesopic tradition, and helpful indices that cross-reference various versions and proper nouns and adjectives that occur within the fables.]

Temple, Richard and Olivia Temple. *The Complete Fables*. New York: Penguin, 1998

[Somewhat of a misnomer, for the Temples' collection only offers translations of the fables (all prose) printed in Chambry's second edition of 1927 (which only selects a single version of a particular fable, unlike Chambry's first edition, which contains multiple variants/versions); for a critical review, see Gibbs (*Bryn Mawr Classical Review*): http://bmcr.brynmawr.edu/1998/98.5.16.html]

OLDER ENGLISH VERSIONS/TRANSLATIONS OF AESOP

Bewick, Thomas. *Bewick's Select fables of Aesop and others. In three parts. 1. Fables extracted from Dodsley's. 2. Fables with reflections in prose and verse. 3. Fables in verse. To which are prefixed The life of Aesop, and An essay upon fable by Oliver Goldsmith*. Newcastle: T. Saint, 1784.

[All indications are that the translations of Aesop employed in this edition are by Oliver Goldsmith (1728-1774). Like Crane's text below, this one puts the illustrator (Bewick) ahead of the translator as 'author.']

Crane, Walter. *The Baby's Own Aesop*. London & New York: George Routledge & Sons, 1887

[Crane's lavishly illustrated edition of fables translated into limericks by W. J. Linton. Recently reprinted in inexpensive paperback editions by Slave Labor Graphics (2014) and Pook Press (2015) that unfortunately diminish the chromatic splendor of the original. For high-quality digital scans of the original text in its entirety, see Gibb's website: http://mythfolklore.net/aesopica/crane/]

L'Estrange, Roger. *Aesop: Fables*. New York: Everyman's Library, 1992

[Includes 192 of the more than 500 fables that Sir Roger L'Estrange first published in 1692; it also includes L'Estrange's translation of *The Life of Aesop*; lastly, it reprints Stephen Gooden's illustrations from the 1936 edition of L'Estrange's translations.]

Jacobs, Joseph. *The Fables of Aesop*. London: Macmillan, 1894

[Includes 82 fables with 170 illustrations by Richard Heighway. Reprinted as an inexpensive paperback by Dover (2002).]

Townsend, George Fyler. *Three Hundred Aesop's Fables. Literally Translated from the Greek. With One Hundred and Fourteen Illustrations, Designed by Harrison Weir and Engraved by J. Greenaway*. London: George Routledge and Sons, 1867

[An influential translation that has gone through many editions.]

English Translations of Fables in the Aesopic Tradition from Latin and French

Phaedrus (c. 15 BCE – c. 50 CE)

Perry, Ben E. (ed.). *Babrius and Phaedrus* (Cambridge, MA: Harvard University Press, 1965)

Odo (c. 1185 – 1246/47)

Jacobs, John. G. (ed.). *The Fables of Odo of Cheriton*. Syracuse, New York: Syracuse University Press, 1985

La Fontaine (1621–1695)

Hill, Craig. *The Complete Fables of La Fontaine: A New Translation in Verse*. New York: Arcade Publishing, 2008

[Lively, contemporary translation infused with a colloquial wit. Several of Hill's translations appear in the selection of comparative fable verisons in this book.]

Shapiro, Norman. *The Complete Fables of Jean de La Fontaine*. Urbana and Chicago: University of Illinois Press, 2007

[This collects together earlier translations of selected La Fontaine fables published by Shapiro in 1985, 1988, and 1998]

Spector, Norman. *The Complete Fables of Jean de La Fontaine*. Evanston, Illinois: Northwestern University Press, 1988

[A bi-lingual edition, with French text on the left and English translation on the right.]

Contemporary Take on the Aesopic Tradition

David Sedaris, *Squirrel Seeks Chipmunk*. New York: Little, Brown and Company, 2010

[An American comic essayist dabbles indirectly in the Aesopic tradition via his encounter with a book of stories from South African mythology about anthropomorphic animals. Sedaris's tales are much longer than a typical fable, and possess a stronger satirical edge.]

Acheson, Katherine O. "The Picture of Nature: Seventeenth-Century English Aesop's Fables." *Journal for Early Modern Cultural Studies*, Vol. 9, No. 2 (Fall 2009): 25-50

Dijk, G.-J. van. *ΑΙΝΟΙ, ΛΟΓΟΙ, ΜΥΘΟΙ: Fables in Archaic, Classical, and Hellenistic Greek Literature: With a Study of the Theory and Terminology of the Genre.* (Mnemosyne, Bibliotheca Classica Batava Supplementum 166) Leiden, The Netherlands: Brill Academic Publishers, 1997

Holzberg, Niklas. "The Fabulist, the Scholars, and the Discourse: Aesop Studies Today." *International Journal of the Classical Tradition* 6 (1999) 236-42.

Kurke, Leslie. "Aesop and the Contestation of Delphic Authority," in Dougherty, C., and Kurke, L., eds., *Cultural Poetics in Archaic Greece: Cult, Performance, Politics.* Oxford: Oxford University Press, 2003: 77-100

————. *Aesopic Conversations: Popular Traditions, Cultural Dialogue, and the Invention of Greek Prose.* Princeton: Princeton University Press, 2011

Lewis, Jayne Elizabeth. *The English Fable: Aesop and Literary Culture, 1651-1740* (Cambridge Studies in Eighteenth-Century English Literature and Thought). Cambridge: Cambridge University Press, 2006

Nagy, Gregory. *The Best of the Achaeans: Concepts of the Hero in Archaic Greek Poetry.* Revised ed. with new introduction. Baltimore: John Hopkins Press, 1999

————. "Diachrony and the Case of Aesop," in González, José M., ed., *Diachrony: Diachronic Studies of Ancient Greek Literature and Culture.* (Berlin: De Gruyter, 2015), 233-290 [online: http://chs.harvard.edu/CHS/article/display/4024]

Patterson, Annabel. *Fables of Power: Aesopian Writing and Political History* (Post-Contemporary Interventions). Durham: Duke University Press, 1991

Zafiropoulos, Christos A. *Ethics in Aesop's Fables: The Augustana Collection* (Mnemosyne, Bibliotheca Classica Batava Supplementum 216). Leiden, The Netherlands: Brill Academic Publishers, 2001

Bibliography - Aesop Illustrated

Artzybasheff, Boris (Illustrator). *Aesop's Fables: Edited and Illustrated with Wood Engravings by Boris Artzybasheff.* New York: Viking Press, 1933

[Stylish images with an intense graphic punch.]

Ash, Russel and B. Highton. *Aesop's Fables: A Classic Illustrated Edition.* San Francisco: Chronicle Books, 1990

[A very generous and beautifully printed selection of the best illustrations from the past 150 years.]

Bennett, Charles H. (Illustrator). *The Fables of Aesop and Others Translated into Human Nature. Designed and Drawn on the Wood by Charles H. Bennett.* London: W. Kent & Co., 1857

[Witty visual transplanting of Aesop's fables into mid-Victorian England; the entire book is digitally available here: www.childrenslibrary.org/]

Calder, Alexander (Illustrator). *Fables of Aesop According to Sir Roger L'Estrange, with Fifty Drawings by Alexander Calder.* Paris: Harrison of Paris, 1931

[Quirky illustrations by the American sculptor, painter, and illustrator famed for his mobiles.]

Condé, J. M. (Illustrator). *Aesop's Fables: An Adaptation of the Translation from the Greek by George F. Townsend.* New York: Moffat, Yard & Company, 1905

[Both ink and water-color illustrations with a sly, whimsical touch; the entire book is digitally available here: www.childrenslibrary.org/]

Detmold, Eward J. (Illustrator). *Fables of Aesop.* London: Hodder & Stoughton, 1909

[Lavishly designed illustrations, often reprinted; the entire book is digitally available here: www.childrenslibrary.org/]

Fiennes, Celia M. (Illustrator). *The Fables of Æsop. Translated by Sir Roger L'Estrange.* (With woodcuts by Celia M. Fiennes.). Waltham St. Lawrence: Golden Cockerel Press, 1926

[11 simple but very powerful illustrations.]

Griset, Ernest Henry (Illustrator). *Aesop's Fables*. London, Paris & New York: Cassell Petter & Galpin, 1874

[Densely designed graphic images; the entire book is digitally available here: www.childrenslibrary.org/]

Heighway, Richard (Illustrator). *The Fables of Aesop. Selected, Told Anew and Their History Traced by Joseph Jacobs. Done into Pictures by Richard Heighway*. London & New York: MacMillan & Co., 1894

[Graphically simple but stylish illustrations; the entire book is digitally available here: www.childrenslibrary.org/]

Lawrence, Jacob. *Aesop's Fables*. Seattle: University of Washington Press, 1997 (reprint, with five additional illustrations, of the 1970 Windmill Books/Simon and Schuster edition)

[Among the most thought-provoking and visually arresting illustrations of Aesop done in the 20th century.]

McKendry, John J. *Aesop Five Centuries of Illustrated Fables*. New York: Metropolitan Museum of Art, 1964

[Excellent survey of Aesopic illustrations with a short but informative introduction on the history of illustrated Aesop editions.]

McTigue, Bernard (translator); Fahy, Everett (introduction). *The Medici Aesop: Spencer MS 50*. New York: Harry N. Abrams, Inc., 1989

[Facsimile-style reproduction with translation of a 15th-century Florentine manuscript of Aesop's fables handwritten in Greek and profusely illustrated.]

Noble, Edwin (Illustrator). *Aesop's Fables*. London: Raphael Tuck & Sons, Ltd., 1912?

[12 beautiful color illustrations, along with numerous black and white ones. Noble did later illustrations of Aesop's fables in 1921, employing a less realistic pictorial mode of color illumination with two differently-sized rectangular segments on a single page.]

Opper, Frederick Burr (Illustrator). *Aesop's Fables with 100 Illustrations by F. Opper*. Philadelphia: J. B. Lippincott and Company, 1916

[Early 20th-century comic-strip style illustrations with a humorous – and occasionally absurdist – twist; the entire text is available here: https://babel.hathitrust.org]

Orr, Jack (Illustrator). *Aesop's Fables Ilustrated By Jack Orr*. London & Edinburgh: Thomas Nelson and Sons, 1927

[Simple yet effective and often droll illustrations.]

Parker, Agnes Miller (Illustrator). *The Fables of Esope*. Gregynog Hall, Powys, Wales: Gregynog Press, 1931.

[Stylish, sophisticated art-nouveau meets modernism woodblock prints.]

Rackham, Arthur (Illustrator), Vernon Jones, V. S. (Translator), and Chesterton, G. K. (Introduction). *Aesop's Fables*. London: Heinemann; New York: Doubleday, 1912

[A famous edition; Rackham's witty and often sophisticated illustrations are perhaps the best known in the English-speaking world.]

Winter, Milo (Illustrator). *Aesop for Children*. Chicago: Rand McNally & Co., 1919

[Beautiful illustrations, often reprinted; the entire book is digitally available here: www.childrenslibrary.org/]

INTERNET RESOURCES

http://www.mythfolklore.net/aesopica/

[Laura Gibb's website contains extensive collections of Greek, Latin, and English texts, translations, and versions, renaissance, early modern, and modern illustrations, and indices that make it easy to search and find fables according to various criteria.]

https://www.creighton.edu/aesop/books/

[Reverend Gregory I. Carlson, S.J. has assembled the most detailed annotated bibliography of Aesop's fables that exists. The texts range from the 1461 Der Edelstein edition up to the most current publications in 2016. Also extremely valuable is Reverend Carlson's discussion of a fable's definition (https://www.creighton.edu/aesop/intro/definition/)]

ABBREVIATIONS

< derived from

acc.(usative)

act.(ive voice)

adj.(ective)

adv.(erb)

aor.(ist)

c. circa

C-to-F = contrary to fact

cf. (*confer*) = compare

Cl. Gk. = Classical Greek (the language as used in the 5th and 4th centuries BCE)

comp.(arative)

condit.(ion)

conj.(unction)

dat.(ive)

dep.(opent)

dir.(ect)

disc.(course)

fem.(inine)

FLV = future less vivid

FMV = future more vivid

fut.(ure)

gen.(itive)

gen.(itive) abs.(olute)

Gk. = Greek (the language as used throughout antiquity and into the Middle Ages)

impera.(tive)

imperf.(ect)

indecl.(inable)

indic.(ative)

indir.(ect)

inf.(initive)

L. Gk. = Later Greek (the language as used from the end of the 4th century BCE up to the Early Middle Ages)

lit.(erally)

masc.(uline)

mid.(dle voice)

neut.(er)

nom.(inative)

obj.(ect)

opt.(ative)

p./pp. page(s)

part.(iciple)
pass.(ive voice)
perf.(ect)
pl.(ural)
pluperf.(ect)
pres.(ent)
pron.(oun)
reflex.(ive) pron.(oun)
rel.(ative) cl.(ause)
rel.(ative) pron.(oun)
sc. *scilicet* (literally, *one may understand, namely*) = supply or understand
sing.(ular)
subj.(ect)
subju.(nctive)
superl.(ative)
trans.(lator)
usu.(ally)
w/ = with

Aesop's
Fables

1. The Murderer
(Chambry 45 [Variant 2] = Perry 32)

Ἄνθρωπός τις φόνον ποιήσας καὶ διωκόμενος ὑπὸ τῶν συγγενῶν τοῦ φονευθέντος κατὰ τὸν Νεῖλον ποταμὸν ἐγένετο καὶ λέοντα εὑρὼν ἀνέβη εἰς δένδρον φοβηθείς, κἀκεῖσε ἰδὼν δράκοντα καὶ ἡμιθνὴς γενόμενος ἔρριψεν
5   ἑαυτὸν εἰς τὸν ποταμόν. Ἐν δὲ τῷ ποταμῷ κροκόδειλος τοῦτον κατεθοινήσατο.

Ὁ λόγος πρὸς τοὺς τῶν ἀνθρώπων φονεῖς ὡς οὔτε γῆ, οὔτε ἀήρ, οὔτε ὕδατος στοιχεῖον, οὔτε ἄλλος τις τόπος φυλάσσει αὐτούς.

---

2   **φονευθέντος** masc. gen. sing. aor. pass. part. < φονεύω
3   **φοβηθείς** masc. nom. sing. aor. pass. (dep.) part. < φοβέομαι
4   **κἀκεῖσε** crasis of καὶ + ἐκεῖσε
7   **Ὁ λόγος** sc. λέγει. The epimythia use either λόγος or μῦθος when referencing the fables. Perry 1936 (171-2) notes that: "In later times μῦθος became so common that it supplanted λόγος..."

Ernst Griset (1874)

2

ἀήρ, ἀέρος, ὁ/ἡ, air
ἄλλος, -ή, -ό, other
ἀναβαίνω, ἀναβήσομαι, ἀνέβην,
  go up, climb
ἄνθρωπος, ὁ, man, person
αὐτός, -ή, -ό, (pron. in gen., dat., acc.)
  him, her, it; them
γί(γ)νομαι, γενήσομαι, ἐγενόμην, be
γῆ, ἡ, earth, land
δένδρον, τό, tree
διώκω, pursue, chase
δράκων, -οντος, ὁ, serpent, snake
ἑαυτοῦ, ἑαυτῆς, ἑαυτοῦ, (refl. pron.
 in gen., dat., acc.) himself, herself, itself;
 themselves
ἐκεῖσε (adv.), there, in that place
εὑρίσκω, εὑρήσω, ηὗρον/εὗρον,
  find
ἡμιθανής/ἡμιθνής -ές, half-dead
κατά (prep. + acc.), by, at, along
καταθοινάω, (mid. w/ same meaning
  as act.) feast on; completely devour
κροκόδειλος, ὁ, crocodile
λέγω, say
λέων, -οντος, ὁ, lion

λόγος, ὁ, story
Νεῖλος, ὁ, Nile
ὁράω, ὄψομαι, εἶδον, see
ὅτι (conj.), that
οὔτε (conj.), neither; οὔτε...οὔτε,
  'neither...nor'
οὗτος, αὕτη, τοῦτο, this; (pl.) these
ποιέω, do, commit
ποταμός, ὁ, river
πρός (prep. + acc.), to
ῥίπτω, throw, hurl; + ἑαυτόν, throw
  or hurl oneself down
στοιχεῖον, τό, element
συγγενής, -οῦς, ὁ, relative
τις, τι (gen. τινος), (indef. adj.) a, an,
  any
τόπος, ὁ, place
ὕδωρ, ὕδατος, τό, water
ὑπό, (prep. + gen.) (w/ pass. voice) by
φοβέομαι (dep.), fear, be or become
  frightened or afraid
φονεύω, murder, kill, slay
φόνος, ὁ, murder
φυλάσσω, keep safe
ὡς (conj.; = ὅτι), that

2. The Fox and the Leopard
(Chambry 37/37 = Perry 12)

Ἀλώπηξ καὶ πάρδαλις περὶ κάλλους ἤριζον. Τῆς δὲ παρδάλεως παρ᾽ ἕκαστα τὴν τοῦ σώματος ποικιλίαν προβαλλομένης, ἡ ἀλώπηξ ὑποτυχοῦσα ἔφη· "Καὶ πόσον ἐγὼ σοῦ καλλίων ὑπάρχω, ἥτις οὐ τὸ σῶμα, τὴν δὲ ψυχὴν
5 πεποίκιλμαι."

Ὁ λόγος δηλοῖ ὅτι τοῦ σωματικοῦ κάλλους ἀμείνων ἐστὶν ὁ τῆς διανοίας κόσμος.

1-2 Τῆς...παρδάλεως...προβαλλομένης gen. abs.

4 σοῦ gen. of comparison (Smyth § 1069); note that in Greek the pron. can precede its comp. adj.
τὸ σῶμα, τὴν...ψύχην acc. of respect x2 (Smyth § 1600)

5 πεποίκιλμαι 1st sing. perf. (often w/ force of pres.) mid./pass. indic. < ποικίλλω

6 τοῦ σωματικοῦ κάλλους gen. of comparison

ἀλώπηξ, -εκος, ἡ, fox
ἀμείνων, -ον, (-ονος, gen.), better
δηλόω, show, reveal
διάνοια, ἡ, thought, intellectual faculty, intelligence, understanding
ἕκαστος, -η, -ον, each one, every one; παρ' ἕκαστα, in every case
ἐρίζω, compete in a contest; debate, argue; + περί τινος, about a thing
καλλίων, -ον, (-ονος, gen.), better, more beautiful, noble or honorable
κάλλος, -εος/ους, τό, beauty
κόσμος ὁ, beautiful/good order or arrangement; ornament
λόγος, ὁ, story, tale
ὅτι (conj.), that
ὅστις, ἥτις, ὅ τι (pron.), (one) who, (one) which or that
πάρδαλις, -εως, ἡ, leopard
περί (prep. + gen.), about, concerning

ποικιλία, ἡ, appearance marked w/ various colors and patterns, spotted appearance; varied aspect, diversity; variety, intricacy, ornamentation
ποικίλλω, make w/ cunning workmanship; embroider; embellish, adorn
πόσον (adv.), how much
προβάλλω, put or bring forward; (mid.) put forward or cite in one's defense
σῶμα, -ματος, τό, body
σωματικός, -ή, -όν, of the body, bodily
ὑπάρχω (= εἰμί), be
ὑποτυγχάνω, ὑποτεύξομαι, ὑπέτυχον, respond, reply
φημί, φήσω, ἔφην (imperf., often w/ aor. force), say
ψυχή, ἡ, soul, spirit, heart, mind

Henry Justice Ford (1888)

5

3. The Fox and the Raven
(Aphthonius 29 = Perry 124)

Μῦθος ὁ τοῦ κόρακος καὶ τῆς ἀλώπεκος παραινῶν
ἀπατῶσι μὴ πείθεσθαι.

Τῷ κόρακι θήραμα τυρὸς ἦν καὶ ἐν μετεώρῳ φέρων
ἐκάθητο. ἰδοῦσα δὲ ἀλώπηξ ἀπάτῃ περιενόστει τὸν κόρακα·
5 "τί ταῦτα;" λέγουσα "μετριότητι μέν, ὦ κόραξ, διενήνοχας
σώματος. χροιὰν δὲ φέρεις τῇ τῶν ὀρνέων ἡγεμονίᾳ
προσήκουσαν· εἰ δὲ καὶ φωνὴ παρῆν, ἅπασαν εἶχες τὴν τῶν
ὀρνίθων ἀρχήν." ταῦτα δὲ εἶπε πρὸς ἀπάτην. ὁ δὲ ὑπαχθείς,
τὸν τυρὸν ἐκβαλών, ἀνέκραγε μέγιστον, φωνῆς ἐπίδειξιν, τὴν
10 ἀφαίρεσιν ποιῶν τοῦ θηράματος. ἡ δὲ λαβοῦσα· "φωνὴ μέν,
ὦ κόραξ," εἶπε "προσῆν, ὁ δὲ νοῦς ἐπιλέλοιπεν."

Ἐχθροῖς πειθαρχῶν ὑποστήσῃ τὴν βλάβην.

1-2 This sentence functions both as title and promythion
1 ὁ τοῦ κόρακος καὶ τῆς ἀλώπεκος in apposition to Μῦθος
παραινῶν sc. us or one
4 ἐκάθητο sc in a tree
ἰδοῦσα fem. nom. sing. aor. act. part. < ὁράω/ὁρῶ
ἀπάτῃ dat. of accompanying circumstance and manner (Smyth § 1527),
i.e., in a deceptive manner
5 τί ταῦτα; lit. 'What (are) these things?', i.e., 'What is this?'
διενήνοχας 2nd sing. perf. act. indic. < διαφέρω; "when the perfect
marks the enduring result rather than the completed act, it may often be
translated by the present" (Smyth § 1946), i.e., you have surpassed = you
are surpassing
7 εἰ...παρῆν,...εἶχες present C-to-F condit. (sc. ἄν in apodosis)
8 ὑπαχθείς masc. nom. sing. aor. pass. part. < ὑπάγω
11 ἐπιλέλοιπεν 3rd sing. perf. act. indic. < ἐπιλείπω
12 πειθαρχῶν ὑποστήσῃ FMV condit., w/ part. as protasis, i.e., if you...
ὑποστήσῃ 2nd sing. fut. mid./pass. indic. < ὑφίστημι

ἀλώπηξ, -εκος, ἡ, fox
ἀνακράζω, ἀνακράξομαι, ἀνέκραγον, cry out, shout
ἅπας, ἅπασα, ἅπαν, whole
ἀπατάω, cheat, trick, deceive
ἀπάτη, ἡ, trick, deceit, stratagem
ἀρχή, ἡ, empire
ἀφαίρεσις, -εως, ἡ, loss
βλάβη, ἡ, harm
διαφέρω, surpass, excel in (+ dat.)
ἐκβάλλω, ἐκβαλῶ, ἐξέβαλον, drop, let fall
ἐπίδειξις, -εως, ἡ, exhibition, display, demonstration; show-off speech
ἐπιλείπω, fail, be defective/lacking
ἐχθρός, ὁ, one's enemy
ἔχω, have
ἡγεμονία, ἡ, presidency, political leadership
θήραμα, -ατος, τό, plunder, spoils
κάθημαι, be seated, sit still/quiet
κόραξ, -ακος, ὁ, raven
λαμβάνω, λήψομαι, ἔλαβον, seize, take
λέγω, λέξω/ἐρῶ, εἶπον, say
μέγιστον (adv.), very loudly
μετέωρον, τό, mid-air
μετριότης, -ητος, ἡ, graceful proportions, elegance

μῦθος, ὁ, story, fable, tale
νοῦς, νοῦ, ὁ, mind, sense, wits
ὁράω/ὁρῶ, ὄψομαι, εἶδον, see
ὄρνεον, τό, bird
ὄρνις, ὄρνιθος, ὁ/ἡ, bird
οὗτος, αὕτη, τοῦτο, this; (pl.) these
παραινέω, exhort, urge, advise
πειθαρχέω, obey, are obedient to, follow (+ dat.)
πείθω, persuade; (mid./pass.) listen to, pay heed to (+ dat.)
περινοστέω, go or walk around; stalk about
ποιέω, bring about, cause
πρός (prep. + acc.), so as to, for the purpose of, in order to
πρόσειμι, προσέσομαι, προσῆν, be there, be present; belong to one (+ dat.)
προσήκω belong to; (part.) belonging to befitting, proper to (+ dat.)
σῶμα, -ατος, τό, body
τυρός, ὁ, cheese
ὑπάγω, lead on/convince by art or deceit
ὑφίστημι, ὑποστήσω, ὑπέστησα, place under; (mid.) bring oneself to
φέρω, bring, carry; bear
φωνή, ἡ, voice
χροιά, ἡ, complexion

How to say 'Go to hell!' in Ancient Greek

Telling someone to 'Go to hell!' in Ancient Greek is literally ἐς κόρακας, 'to the ravens.' This expression occurs several times in the comedies of the playwright Aristophanes (c. 446 - c. 386 BCE). Two examples follow:

βάλλ' ἐς κόρακας, 'Throw (yourself) to the ravens!' (*Clouds* 133)
ἀπόφερ' ἐς κόρακας, 'Take (yourself) away to the ravens!' (*Peace* 133)

L'Estrange (1692)

A certain *Fox* spy'd out a *Raven*, upon a Tree with a Morsel in his Mouth, that set his Chops a watering: but how to come at it was the Question. Oh thou blessed Bird! (says he) the Delight of the Gods and of Men! and so he lays himself forth upon the Gracefulness of the *Raven*'s Person, and the Beauty of his Plumes: his admirable Gift of *Augury*, &c. and now, says the *Fox*, if thou hast but a Voice answerable to the rest of thy excellent Qualities, the Sun in the Firmament could not shew the World such another Creature. This nauseous Flattery sets the *Raven* immediately a gaping as wide as he ever could stretch, to give the *Fox* a taste of his Pipe; but upon the opening of his Mouth, he drops his Breakfast, which the *Fox* presently chopt up, and then bad him remember, that whatever he had said of his *Beauty*, he had spoken nothing yet out of his *Brains*.

THE MORAL. *There's hardly any Man living that may not be wrought upon more or less by Flattery: For we do all of us naturally overween in our own Favour? But when it comes to be applied once to a vain Fool, it makes him forty times an arranter Sot than he was before.*

Agnes Miller Parker (1931)

8

Jacob Lawrence (1970)
[© 2016 The Jacob and Gwendolyn Knight Lawrence Foundation,
Seattle / Artists Rights Society (ARS), New York]

Alexander Calder (1931)

Richard Heighway (1894)

4. The Wolf, the Fox, and the Sick Lion
(Chambry 206/205 = Perry 258)

Λέων γηράσας ἐνόσει κατακεκλιμένος ἐν ἄντρῳ.
Παρῆσαν δ' ἐπισκεψόμενα τὸν βασιλέα, πλὴν ἀλώπεκος,
τἄλλα τῶν ζώων. Ὁ τοίνυν λύκος λαβόμενος εὐκαιρίας
κατηγόρει παρὰ τῷ λέοντι τῆς ἀλώπεκος, ἅτε δὴ παρ'
οὐδὲν τιθέμενης τὸν πάντων αὐτῶν κρατοῦντα, καὶ διὰ
5   ταῦτα μηδ' εἰς ἐπίσκεψιν ἀφιγμένης. Ἐν τοσούτῳ δὲ παρῆν
καὶ ἡ ἀλώπηξ, καὶ τῶν τελευταίων ἠκροάσατο τοῦ λύκου
ῥημάτων. Ὁ μὲν οὖν λέων κατ' αὐτῆς ἐβρυχᾶτο. Ἡ δ'
ἀπολογίας καιρὸν αἰτήσασα· "Καὶ τίς σε," ἔφη, "τῶν
συνελθόντων τοσοῦτον ὠφέλησεν ὅσον ἐγώ, πανταχόσε
10   περινοστήσασα, καὶ θεραπείαν ὑπὲρ σοῦ παρ' ἰατρῶν
ζητήσασα καὶ μαθοῦσα;" Τοῦ δὲ λέοντος εὐθὺς τὴν
θεραπείαν εἰπεῖν κελεύσαντος, ἐκείνη φησίν· "Εἰ λύκον
ζῶντα ἐκδείρας τὴν αὐτοῦ δορὰν θερμὴν ἀμφιέσῃ." Καὶ
τοῦ λύκου αὐτίκα νεκροῦ κειμένου, ἡ ἀλώπηξ γελῶσα
15   εἶπεν οὕτως· "Οὐ χρὴ τὸν δεσπότην πρὸς δυσμένειαν
παρακινεῖν, ἀλλὰ πρὸς εὐμένειαν."

[Continued on page 14]

---

1   γηράσας masc. nom. sing. aor. act. part. < γηράσκω/γηράω
      κατακεκλιμένος masc. nom. sing. perf. mid./pass. part. < κατακλίνω
2-3   Παρῆσαν...ζώων = δ' πλὴν ἀλώπεκος, τἄλλα τῶν ζώων παρῆσαν
      ἐπισκεψόμενα τὸν βασιλέα. For neut. pl. subj. (τἄλλα = τὰ + ἄλλα) w/ pl.
      vb. (normally neut. pl. subj. governs sing. vb.), see Smyth § 959
      ἐπισκεψόμενα fut. part., w/ or w/out ὡς, expresses purpose (Smyth § 2065)
4   τὸν...κρατοῦντα substantive noun phrase (article + part.)
5   ἀφιγμένης fem. gen. sing. perf. mid./pass. part. < ἀφικνέομαι
9   συνελθόντων neut. gen. pl. aor. act. part. < συνέρχομαι
11-12 Τοῦ δὲ λέοντος...κελεύσαντος gen. abs.
12-13 Εἰ...ἀμφιέσῃ protasis of an 'emotional' FMV condit., w/ εἰ + fut. indic. in
      place of ἐάν, + subju. (Smyth § 2328); sc. for apodosis 'you will be cured'
14   τοῦ λύκου...νεκροῦ κειμένου gen. abs.

αἰτέω, ask for (+ acc.)
ἀκροάομαι, listen to, hear (+ gen.)
ἄλλος, -η, -ο, another; (+ pl. article)
    all the others, the rest
ἀλώπηξ, ἀλώπεκος, ἡ, fox
ἀμφιέννυμι, ἀμφιέσω, ἠμφιεσάμην,
    put round or on; (mid.) put on oneself
ἄντρον, τό, cave
ἀπολογία, ἡ, defense speech
ἅτε (adv. + part.), inasmuch as, seeing that
αὐτίκα (adv.), at once, immediately
αὐτός, -ή, -ό, (pron. in gen., dat., acc.)
    him, her, it; them
ἀφικνέομαι, (+ εἰς) come to
βασιλεύς, -έως, ὁ, king
βρυχάομαι, roar
γελάω, laugh
γηράσκω/γηράω, grow or become old
δεσπότης, -ου, ὁ, master
δή (particle), now, in truth, indeed
διά, (prep. + acc.) because of; + τοῦτο/
    ταῦτα, therefore
δορά, ἡ, skin, hide
δυσμένεια, ἡ, ill-will, enmity
εἰ (conj.), if
εἰς (prep. + acc., of purpose or object),
    for; εἰς ἐπίσκεψιν, to visit
ἐκδέρω, ἐκδερῶ, ἐκέδειρα, strip off
    the skin from (one), flay, skin
ἐκεῖνος, -η, -ο, that (one/thing)
ἐπίσκεψις, -εως, ἡ, visit
ἐπισκοπέω, ἐπισκέψομαι,
    ἐπεσκεψάμην, look upon; visit
εὐθύς (adv.), at once, immediately
εὐκαιρία, ἡ, opportunity
εὐμένεια, ἡ, goodwill
ζητέω, seek, seek for; enquire
ζῶ, live
ζῷον/ζῶον, τό, living being, animal
θεραπεία, ἡ, cure, remedy
θερμός, -ή, -όν, hot, warm; still warm
ἰατρός, ὁ, doctor
καιρός, ὁ, opportunity
λέγω, λέξω/ἐρῶ, εἶπον, say
κατά (prep. + gen.), at or against (in
    hostile sense)

κατακλίνω, lay down
κατηγορέω, denounce X (gen.)
κεῖμαι, lie
κελεύω, urge, order, command
κρατέω, be lord or master of, rule
    over (+ gen.)
λαμβάνω, λήψομαι, ἔλαβον, take;
    (mid.) take hold of, seize (+ gen.)
λέων, -οντος, ὁ, lion
λύκος, ὁ, wolf
μανθάνω, μαθήσομαι, ἔμαθον,
    learn
μηδέ (adv.), not even
νεκρός, -ή, -όν, dead
νοσέω, be sick
ὅσον (adv.), as/so much as
ὅτι (conj.), that
οὕτως (adv.), so, thus
πανταχόσε (adv.), everywhere
παρά (prep. + gen.), from; (+ dat.),
    before, in the presence of; (+ acc.
    w/ vbs. of estimating) equivalent to
παρακινέω, incite, stir up
πάρειμι, be present
πᾶς, πᾶσα, πᾶν, all, every
περινοστέω, go around
πλήν (prep. + dat.) except for
ῥῆμα, -ατος, τό, that which is said
    or spoken, word
σύνειμι, be with (+ dat.)
συνέρχομαι, come together, assemble
τελευταῖος, -α, -ον, last
τίθημι, reckon or regard as
τίς, τί (gen. τίνος; interrog. pron. and
    adj.), who? which? what?; ?; τί, 'why'?
τοίνυν (inferential particle), therefore
τοσοῦτος, -αύτη, -οῦτο, so great;
    ἐν τοσούτῳ, in the meantime;
    τοσοῦτον (adv.), so much
ὑπέρ (prep. + gen.), for the sake of,
    for, on behalf of
φημί, φήσω, ἔφην, say
χρή, one must or ought (+ inf.)
ὠφελέω, help

4. The Wolf, the Fox, and the Sick Lion - Continued
(Chambry 206/205 = Perry 258)

Ὁ μῦθος δηλοῖ ὅτι ὁ καθ' ἑτέρου μηχανώμενος καθ' ἑαυτοῦ τὴν μηχανὴν περιτρέπει.

δηλόω, show, reveal

ἑαυτοῦ, -ῆς, -οῦ (reflex. pron. in gen., dat., acc.), himself, herself, itself; themselves

ἕτερος, -η, -ον, another

κατά (prep. + gen.), at or against (in hostile sense)

μηχανῶμαι, plot, devise, scheme

μηχανή, ἡ, plot, scheme

μῦθος, ὁ, story, fable, tale

ὅτι (conj.), that

περιτρέπω, turn and bring around

La Fontaine (1668)
(trans. Hill [2008])

Decrepit, gouty, hardly able still to hobble,
A lion wished to have a cure for old age found.
To tell a king that something is impossible
Is never wise, so orders went around
That every species had to send
A physician to attend
His Highness – and they came, doctors of all descriptions,
Prepared to dose him with prescriptions,
All but the fox, who stayed holed up though not excused.
With fox away from court, the wolf abused
His absent comrade in the monarch's ears,
And soon the offended lion made it loudly known
That Fox must be smoked out and summoned to appear
Before him. This was done. Fox came before the throne,
Certain he saw the wolf's influence here.
"Your majesty," he said, "I fear a false report
May have been spread about my absence from the court.
The truth is, Sire, I was away
Upon a pilgrimage to pray
For your good health. And I found experts to consult
While traveling, who said there is a way to treat

14

This languor that, neglected, might, one fears, result
In grave effects. They said a simple loss of heat
Through age has caused the symptoms you have felt.
The cure is simple, too. You take the pelt,
All hot and reeking, from a wolf fresh-skinned alive
And wrap it close around you. The heat you thus derive
Is a most sovereign remedy for age's chill.
That nice Sir Wolf, should you so will,
Can serve your majesty as royal dressing gown."
The lion was pleased by this advice;
The wolf was seized and in a trice
Was flayed, dismembered, carved, and taken down
To bite-sized bits. The monarch dined on wolf ragout
And wore wolf fur around him, too.
Politicians, cease destroying one another;
Try to be statesmen, not assassins of each other.
Your evil deeds outweigh your good by four on one,
But to evildoers evil will be done.
The beckoning path on which you're driven
Ends in a place where none's forgiven.

5a. The Fox and the Grapes
(Chambry 32/32 = Perry 15)

Ἀλώπηξ λιμώττουσα, ὡς ἐθεάσατο ἀπό τινος ἀναδενδράδος βότρυας κρεμαμένους, ἠβουλήθη αὐτῶν περιγενέσθαι καὶ οὐκ ἠδύνατο. Ἀπαλλαττομένη δὲ πρὸς ἑαυτὴν εἶπεν· "Ὄμφακές εἰσιν."

5 Οὕτω καὶ τῶν ἀνθρώπων ἔνιοι τῶν πραγμάτων ἐφικέσθαι μὴ δυνάμενοι δι' ἀσθένειαν τοὺς καιροὺς αἰτιῶνται.

---

2 **αὐτῶν** if *περιγενέσθαι* has here a L. Gk. meaning, then this is partitive gen. (Smyth § 1341), i.e., '(some) of them'

3 **περιγενέσθαι** if Cl. Gk. in meaning, then this is comically over the top

4 **Ὄμφακές** The Temples (*The Complete Fables* [New York: 1998, 32]) note that: "This famous fable gave rise to the common English expression 'Sour grapes.' *Omphakes* can mean 'sour', but it is more accurate to translate it as 'unripe', since the sourness was a result of the unripeness, and when Greeks used the word to describe grapes they were usually referring to their unripe state rather than to their taste. The same word was used to describe girls who had not yet reached sexual maturity."

5 **τῶν ἀνθρώπων** partitive gen. w/ *ἔνιοι*, 'some men' (Smyth § 1306)

6 **μὴ** + part. is equivalent to a conditional cl. (Smyth § 2728)

5b. The Fox and the Grapes
(Chambry 32 [Variant 2] = Perry 15)

Βότρυας πεπείρους ἀλώπηξ κρεμαμένους ἰδοῦσα, τούτους ἐπειρᾶτο καταφαγεῖν· πολλὰ δὲ καμοῦσα καὶ μὴ δυνηθεῖσα ψαῦσαι, τὴν λύπην παραμυθουμένη ἔλεγεν· "Ὄμφακες ἔτι εἰσιν."

5 Τοὺς δι' ἀδυναμίαν τινὸς ἀποτυγχάνοντας πράγματος καὶ θέλοντας τοῦτο διὰ ψεύδους καλύψαι ἐλέγχει ὁ μῦθος.

---

1 **ἰδοῦσα** fem. nom. sing. aor. act. part. < *ὁράω/ὁρῶ*

2 **καμοῦσα** fem. nom. sing. aor. act. part. < *κάμνω*; here w/ causal force (so too *μὴ δυνηθεῖσα* [for the use of *μὴ* + part., see Smyth § 2731])

3 **ἔλεγεν** note change in tense from previous version

5-6 **Τοὺς...ἐλέγχει ὁ μῦθος** note word order

ἀδυναμία, ἡ, weakness, inability, powerlessness, lack of power or strength

αἰτιάομαι/αἰτιῶμαι, blame

ἀλώπηξ, -εκος, ἡ, fox

ἀναδενδράς, -άδος, ἡ, vine that grows up trees

ἄνθρωπος, ὁ, man, person, human being

ἀπαλλάσσω/ἀπαλλάττω, set free; (mid./pass.) depart, go away

ἀποτυγχάνω, fail to obtain X (gen.)

ἀσθένεια, ἡ, weakness

αὐτός, -ή, -ό, (pron. in gen., dat., acc.) him, her, it; them

βότρυς, -υος, ὁ, bunch of grapes; (pl.) grapes

βούλομαι (aor. and imperf. often w/ double augment, i.e., ἠβ- in place of ἐβ-), want or wish to (+ inf.)

διά (prep. + acc.), because of, on account of

δύναμαι, be able to (+ inf.)

ἑαυτοῦ, -ῆς, -οῦ (reflex. pron. in gen., dat., acc.), himself, herself, itself; themselves

ἐλέγχω, reproach

ἔνιοι, -αι, -α, some

ἔτι (adv.), still

ἐφικνέομαι, ἐφίξομαι, ἐφικόμην, reach, attain (+ gen.)

θεάομαι, see

θέλω/ἐθέλω, want or wish to (+ inf.)

καιρός, ὁ, time, season; οἱ καιροί, lit., the times, i.e., the state of affairs, circumstances

καλύπτω, καλύψω, ἐκάλυψα, hide, conceal

κάμνω, καμοῦμαι, ἔκαμον, grow tired, be/become weary or exhausted

κατεσθίω, κατέδομαι, κατέφαγον, eat up, devour

κρεμάννυμι, hang up; (pass.) be hung up, suspended; (pass. part.) hanging

λέγω, λέξω/ἐρῶ, εἶπον, say

λιμώσσω/λιμώττω, be famished or hungry

λύπη, ἡ, grief, anguish; sad plight

μῦθος, ὁ, story, fable, tale

ὄμφαξ, -ακος, ἡ, unripe grape

ὁράω/ὁρῶ, ὄψομαι, εἶδον, see

οὗτος, αὕτη, τοῦτο, this; (pl.) these

οὕτω/οὕτως (adv.), so, in this way

παραμυθέομαι, assuage

πειράομαι, attempt, try (+ inf.)

πέπειρος, -ον, ripe

περιγί(γ)νομαι, περιγενήσομαι, περιεγενόμην, (L. Gk.) get, take; (Cl. Gk.) be superior to, overcome, prevail over (+ gen.)

πολύς, πολλή, πολύ, much; (pl.) many; πολλά (adv.), very

πρᾶγμα, -ατος, τό, thing or matter of consequence or importance; (pl. can also mean) power, supremacy, political power

τις, τι, (gen. τινος) (indef. adj.) a certain; some; a, an; (indef. pron.) someone; something; anyone; anything

ψαύω, reach

ψεῦδος, -εος/ους, τό, lie, falsehood

ὡς (+ indic. past tense vb.), when

Richard Heighway (1894)

L'Estrange (1692)

There was a Time when a *Fox* would have ventur'd as far for a Bunch of *Grapes* as for a Shoulder of Mutton; and it was a *Fox* of those Days, and that Palate, that stood gaping under a Vine, and licking his Lips at a most delicious Cluster of Grapes that he had spy'd out there; he fetch'd a hundred and a hundred Leaps at it, till at last, when he was as weary as a Dog, and found that there was no Good to be done; *Hang 'em* (says he) *they are as sour as Crabs*; and so away he went, turning off the Disappointment with a Jest.

THE MORAL OF THE TWO FABLES ABOVE.[6] *'Tis Matter of Skill and Address, when a Man cannot honestly compass what he would be at, to appear easy and indifferent upon all Repulses and Disappointments.*

Goldsmith (1784)

A Fox, very hungry, chanced to come into a Vineyard, where there hung many bunches of charming ripe grapes; but nailed up to a trellis so high, that he leaped till he quite tired himself without being able to reach one of them. At last, Let who will take them! says he; but they are but green and sour; so I'll even let them alone.

MORALS.

When a man finds it impossible to obtain the things he longs for, it is a mark of sound wisdom and discretion to make a virtue of necessity.

> *Old maids who loathe the matrimonial state,*
> *Poor rogues who laugh to scorn the rich and great,*
> *Patriots who rail at placemen and at pow'r,*
> *All, like sly* Reynard, *say* "The Grapes are sour."

---

[6] L'Estrange pairs the fable of the Fox and the Grapes with that of the Wolf and the Lion (not included in the selections of this text), and gives them a joint moral.

REFLECTION.

This Fable is a good reprimand to a parcel of vain coxcombs in the world, who, because they would never be thought to be disappointed in any of their pursuits, pretend a dislike to everything which they cannot obtain. There is a strange propensity in mankind to this temper, and there are numbers of grumbling malcontents in every different faculty and sect in life. The discarded statesman, considering the corruption of the times, would not have any hand in the administration of affairs for all the world. The country squire damns a court life, and would not go cringing and creeping to a drawing-room for the best place the King has in his disposal. A young fellow, being asked how he liked a celebrated beauty, by whom all the world knew he was despised, answered, "She had a stinking breath." How insufferable is the pride of this poor creature man! who would stoop to the basest, vilest actions, rather than be thought not able to do anything. For what is more base and vile than lying? And when do we lie more notoriously, than when we disparage and find fault with a thing for no other reason but because it is out of our power.

Linton (1887)

This Fox has a longing for grapes,
He jumps, but the bunch still escapes.
So he goes away sour;
And, 'tis said, to this hour
Declares that he's no taste for grapes.

THE GRAPES OF DISAPPOINTMENT ARE ALWAYS SOUR

Jacobs (1894)

One hot summer's day a Fox was strolling through an orchard till he came to a bunch of Grapes just ripening on a vine which had been trained over a lofty branch. "Just the thing to quench my thirst," quoth he. Drawing back a few paces, he took a run and a jump, and just missed the bunch. Turning round again with a One, Two, Three, he jumped up, but with no greater success. Again and again he tried after the tempting morsel, but at last had to give it up, and walked away with his nose in the air, saying: "I am sure they are sour."

It is easy to despise what you cannot get.

Alexander Calder (1931)

Boris Artzybasheff (1933)

6. The Fisherman and the Little Fish
(Chambry 26 = Perry 18)

Ἁλιεὺς καθεὶς τὸ δίκτυον ἀνήνεγκε μαινίδα. Τῆς δὲ
ἱκετευούσης αὐτὸν πρὸς τὸ παρὸν μεθεῖναι αὐτήν, ἐπειδὴ
μικρὰ τυγχάνει, ὕστερον δὲ αὐξηθεῖσαν συλλαμβάνειν εἰς
μείζονα ὠφέλειαν, ὁ ἁλιεὺς εἶπεν· "Ἀλλ' ἐγὼ εὐηθέστατος
5 ἂν εἴην, εἰ τὸ ἐν χειρὶ παρεὶς κέρδος, ἄδηλον ἐλπίδα
διώκοιμι."

Ὁ λόγος δηλοῖ ὅτι αἱρετώτερόν ἐστι τὸ παρὸν κέρδος,
κἂν μικρὸν ᾖ, ἢ τὸ προσδοκώμενον, κἂν μέγα ὑπάρχῃ.

---

1 καθεὶς masc. nom. sing. aor. act. part. < καθίημι
2-3 Τῆς...ἱκετευούσης gen. abs.
2 μεθεῖναι aor. act. inf. < μεθίημι
3 αὐξηθεῖσαν fem. acc. sing. aor. pass. part. < αὐξάνω
5-6 ἂν εἴην, εἰ...διώκοιμι FLV condit.; both εἴην (< εἰμί) and διώκοιμι are
1st. sing. pres. opt.
5 παρεὶς masc. nom. sing. aor. act. part. < παρίημι
7-8 ἐστι...κἂν...ᾖ...κἂν...ὑπάρχῃ pres. general condit.; both ᾖ (< εἰμί) and
ὑπάρχῃ are 3rd sing. pres. act. subju.
8 κἂν = καὶ + ἂν (= ἐὰν [εἰ + ἂν]), 'even if' (+ subju.)

ἄδηλος, -ον, uncertain, unknown

αἱρετός, -ή, -όν, be chosen, preferable

ἁλιεύς, -έως, ὁ, fisherman

ἀναφέρω, ἀνοίσω, ἀνήνεγκα, bring up

αὐξάνω, increase; (pass.) grow, increase, grow up

αὐτός, -ή, -ό, (pron. in gen., dat., acc.) him, her, it; them

δηλόω, show, reveal

δίκτυον, τό, net

διώκω, pursue, seek (after)

εἰς (prep. + acc. of purpose or object), for

ἐλπίς, -ίδος, ἡ, hope, expectation

ἐπειδή (conj.), since

εὐήθης, -ες, simple-minded, foolish, naive

ἤ (conj.; w/ comp.), than

ἱκετεύω, beseech or beg X (acc.) to do Y (inf.)

καθίημι, καθήσω, καθῆκα, let down, lower

κέρδος, -εος, τό, gain, profit

λέγω, λέξω/ἐρῶ, εἶπον, say

λόγος, ὁ, story, tale

μαινίς, -ίδος, ἡ, sprat (any of various small, herring-like marine fish in the genus Sprattus, in the family Clupeidae)

μέγας, μεγάλη, μέγα, great, big

μεθίημι, release, let go

μείζων, -ον, (-ονος, gen.), greater, bigger

μικρός, -ά, -όν, small, little

ὅτι (conj.), that

πάρειμι, be present, be at hand; τὸ παρόν, the present time/moment

παρίημι, give up; let fall

πρός (prep. + acc.), at [of time]

προσδοκάω, expect, look for; τὸ προσδοκώμενον, that which is expected or hoped for

συλλαμβάνω, seize, lay hold of

τυγχάνω, happen to be, be

ὑπάρχω (= εἰμί), be

ὕστερον (adv.), later, afterwards

χείρ, χειρός (poetic), ἡ, hand

ὠφέλεια, ἡ, profit, benefit, use

Richard Heighway (1894)

Jacob Lawrence (1970)
[© 2016 The Jacob and Gwendolyn Knight Lawrence Foundation,
Seattle / Artists Rights Society (ARS), New York]

7. The Old Man and Death
(Chambry 78 = Perry 60)

Γέρων ποτὲ ξύλα κόψας καὶ ταῦτα φέρων πολλὴν ὁδὸν ἐβάδιζε. Διὰ δὲ τὸν κόπον τῆς ὁδοῦ ἀποθέμενος τὸ φορτίον τὸν Θάνατον ἐπεκαλεῖτο. Τοῦ δὲ Θανάτου φανέντος καὶ πυθομένου δι' ἣν αἰτίαν αὐτὸν παρακαλεῖται, ὁ γέρων ἔφη·

5   "Ἵνα τὸ φορτίον ἄρῃς."

Ὁ μῦθος δηλοῖ ὅτι πᾶς ἄνθρωπος φιλόζωος, ἐν τῷ βίῳ κἂν δυστυχῇ.

---

2   τῆς ὁδοῦ obj. gen., i.e. 'caused by...' (Smyth § 1331, 1332)
3-4 Τοῦ...Θανάτου φανέντος καὶ πυθομένου gen. abs. x2
3   φανέντος masc. gen. sing. aor. pass. part. < φαίνω
4   δι' ἣν αἰτίαν lit., 'on account of which reason?', i.e., why?
7   κἂν = καὶ + ἂν (= ἐὰν [εἰ + ἂν]), 'even if' (+ subju.)

8. The Poor Man and Death
(Syntipas 2 = Perry 60)

Ἄνθρωπός τις ἦν πένης, ὃς καὶ ξύλων γόμον ἐπὶ τῶν νώτων ἐβάσταζε. κατὰ δὲ τὴν ὁδοιπορίαν ἰλιγγιάσας ἐκαθέσθη καὶ τὸν γόμον κατέθετο καὶ τὸν Θάνατον οἰκτρῶς ἐνεκαλεῖτο, λέγων "ὦ Θάνατε." αὐτίκα γοῦν ὁ Θάνατος

5   ἔφθασε καὶ πρὸς αὐτὸν ἔφη "τίνος χάριν ἐκάλεσάς με;" λέγει πρὸς αὐτὸν ὁ ἀνήρ "ἵνα τὸν γόμον ἀπὸ τῆς γῆς συνεξάρῃς μοι."

Οὗτος δηλοῖ ὅτι πάντες ἄνθρωποι φιλόζωοι τυγχάνουσιν, εἰ καὶ θλίψεσι καὶ ἀνάγκαις συνέχονται.

---

3   ἐκαθέσθη 3rd sing. aor. pass. (dep.). indic. < καθέζομαι
     κατέθετο 3rd sing. aor. mid. indic. < κατατίθημι
8   Οὗτος = Οὗτος μῦθος/λόγος

αἴρω, ἀρῶ, ἦρα, lift, raise up; take up, take up and carry/bring, bring, bear (a burden)

αἰτία, ἡ, cause, reason

ἀνάγκη, ἡ, pain, anguish, distress

ἄνθρωπος, ὁ, man, person, human being

ἀνήρ, ἀνδρός, ὁ, man, husband

ἀποτίθημι, put away; (mid.) set/put down

αὐτίκα (adv.), at once, immediately

αὐτός, -ή, -ό, (pron. in gen., dat., acc.) him, her, it; them

βαδίζω, go (slowly)

βαστάζω, carry

βίος, ὁ, life

γέρων, -οντος, ὁ, old man

γῆ, ἡ, ground

γόμος, ὁ, load (usu. a load carried by beasts of burden)

γοῦν (particle), οὖν ('then') + γε (putting emphasis on the word that precedes it, often only to be rendered by italics in writing, or emphasis in pronunciation)

διά (prep. + acc.), because of

δηλόω, show, reveal

δυστυχέω, be unlucky, unhappy, or unfortunate

ἐγκαλέω, (act./mid.) call upon, appeal to, entreat

εἰ (conj.), if

ἐπικαλέω, invoke; invite; (mid.) call in (as a helper or ally), summon

Θάνατος, ὁ, Death

θλῖψις, -εως, ἡ, oppression, affliction

ἰλιγγιάω, become dizzy, grow faint

ἵνα (conj. + subju.), that, so that, in order that

καθέζομαι, sit down

καλέω, call, summon

κατά (prep. + acc.) on

κατατίθημι, (act./mid.) put or lay down

κόπος, ὁ, fatigue, weariness

κόπτω, chop

λέγω, λέξω/ἐρῶ, εἶπον, say

λόγος, ὁ, tale, story

μῦθος, ὁ, story, fable, tale

νῶτον, -ου, τό, back; (pl.) back, shoulders

ξύλον, τό, (single piece of) wood; (pl.) firewood

ὁδοιπορία, ἡ, journey

ὁδός, ὁδοῦ, ἡ, road, way, journey

οἰκτρῶς (adv.), wailing piteously, in a pitiful or miserable way, pitifully, miserably

ὅς, ἥ, ὅ (rel. pron.), who, whose, whom, which, that

ὅτι (conj.), that

οὗτος, αὕτη, τοῦτο, this; (pl.) these

παρακαλέω, (act./mid.) call

πᾶς, πᾶσα, πᾶν, all, every

πένης, -ητος, ὁ, one who works for his daily bread, day-laborer, poor man; (as adj.) poor

πολύς, πολλή, πολύ, much; (pl.) many; + ὁδός, a long way

ποτε (adv.), at one time, once (upon a time)

πυνθάνομαι, πεύσομαι, ἐπυθόμην, inquire, ask

συνεξαίρω, συνεξαρῶ, συνεξῆρα, help lift up, assist in raising

συνέχω, constrain, oppress; (pass.) be trapped; be distressed or afflicted

τις, τι, (gen. τινος) (indef. adj.) a certain, some; a, an

τίς, τί (gen. τίνος; interrog. pron. and adj.), who? which? what?

τυγχάνω, happen to be, be

φαίνω, bring to light; (pass.) appear

φέρω, carry

φημί, φήσω, ἔφην, say

φθάνω, φθήσομαι, ἔφθασα, come (to)

φιλόζωος, -ον, fond of (one's) life

φορτίον, τό, load, burden

χάριν (prep. + gen.), for the sake of, on behalf of, on account of; + τίνος, for what reason?, why?

Goldsmith (1784)

A poor feeble old man, who had crawled out into a neighbouring wood to gather a few sticks, had made up his bundle, and, laying it over his shoulders, was trudging homeward with it; but, what with age, and the length of the way, and the weight of his burden, he grew so faint and weak that he sunk under it; and, as he sat on the ground, called upon Death to come, once for all, and ease him of his troubles. Death no sooner heard him, but he came and demanded of him what he wanted. The poor old creature, who little thought Death had been so near, and frightened almost out of his senses with his terrible aspect, answered him trembling: That having by chance let his bundle of sticks fall, and being too infirm to get it up himself, he had made bold to call upon him to help him; that, indeed, this was all he wanted at present; and that he hoped his Worship was not offended with him for the liberty he had taken in so doing.

MORALS.

Men under calamity may seem to wish for death; but they seldom bid him welcome when he stares them in the face.

" Oh with what joy I resign my breath! "
The wretch exclaims, and prays for instant death:
The fiend approaching, he inverts his pray'r,
" Oh grant me life, and double all my care! "

REFLECTION.

This Fable gives us a lively representation of the general behavior of mankind towards the grim king of terrors, Death. Such liberties do they take with him behind his back, that upon every little cross accident which happens in their way, Death is immediately called upon; and they even wish it might be lawful for them to finish by their own hands a life so odious, so perpetually tormenting and vexatious. When, let but Death only offer to make his appearance, and the very sense of his near approach almost does the business: Oh then, all they want is a longer life; and they would be glad to come off so well, as to have their old burden laid upon their shoulders again. One may well conclude what an utter aversion they, who are in youth, health, and vigour of body, have to dying, when age, poverty, and wretchedness, are not sufficient to reconcile us to the thought.

Dutch Woodcut (1727)

William Mulready (1807)

Richard Heighway (1894)

Frederick Burr Opper (1916)

Anonymous (1916)[7]

An old, old man had nobody to gather wood for his fire so he had to hobble out into the wood himself and gather up all the sticks he could find. After he had tied them into a bundle he started home, but soon he sank to the ground with the terrible weight on his back. In his fright he called aloud, "I want to die. Come, Death, and end my troubles."

No sooner were the words uttered than Death answered, "Did you call me, old Man? Here I am."

Now of course the old Man did not really want to die so he was hard put to for an excuse.

"Well, Death," he said, trembling, "won't you please help me home; pick up my bundle? You are so strong and I am only a weak old Man."

---

[7] From *Aesop's Fables with 100 Illustrations by F. Opper* (Philadelphia: J. B. Lippincott Company, 1916).

Frederick Burr Opper (1916)

Death had a feeling that he was being cheated, but he lent a hand and got the bundle on the old Man's back again; then Death watched him till he got to his shack.

MORAL: Death really does have a tough time: Everybody tries so hard to elude him.

Frederick Burr Opper (1916)

9. Zeus and the Tortoise
(Chambry 126 [Variant 2] = Perry 106)

Ζεὺς γάμους τελῶν πάντα τὰ ζῷα εἱστία· Μόνης δὲ τῆς χελώνης ὑστερησάσης, διαπορῶν τὴν αἰτίαν τῆς ὑστερήσεως, ἐπυνθάνετο αὐτῆς τίνος χάριν αὐτὴ ἐπὶ τὸ δεῖπνον οὐ παρεγένετο. Τῆς δὲ εἰπούσης· "Οἶκος φίλος,

5   οἶκος ἄριστος," ἀγανακτήσας κατ' αὐτῆς κατεδίκασε τὸν οἶκον βαστάζουσαν περιφέρειν.

Ὁ μῦθος δηλοῖ ὅτι οἱ πολλοὶ τῶν ἀνθρώπων αἱροῦνται μᾶλλον λιτῶς παρ' ἑαυτοῖς ζῆν ἢ παρ' ἄλλοις πολυτελῶς.

---

1   εἱστία 3rd sing. imperf. act. indic. < ἑστιάω

1-2   Μόνης...χελώνης ὑστερησάσης gen. abs.

2   διαπορῶν subj. is Zeus

4   Τῆς...εἰπούσης gen. abs.

4-5   Οἶκος φίλος, οἶκος ἄριστος sc. ἐστί for each clause. Cf. English, "Be it ever so humble, there is no place like home."

5   κατεδίκασε instead of gen. as obj. of this vb. (perhaps on account of desire to avoid repetition w/ prep. phrase κατ' αὐτῆς), the obj. is acc. βαστάζουσαν (i.e., αὐτήν βαστάζουσαν)

6   βαστάζουσαν περιφέρειν note repetition of verbal meaning for emphasis

---

L'Estrange (1692)

When the Toy had once taken Jupiter in the Head to enter into a State of Matrimony, he resolv'd, for the Honour of his Celestial Lady, that the whole World should keep a *Festival* upon the Day of his Marriage, and so Invited all Living Creatures, *Tag, Rag, and Bob-tail*, to the Solemnity of the Wedding. They all came in very good Time, saving only the *Tortoise*. *Jupiter* told him 'twas ill done to make the Company Stay, and ask'd him, Why so late? Why truly, says the *Tortoise*, I was at Home, at my Own House, my dearly Beloved House, and [*Home is Home let it be never so Homely.*] *Jupiter* took it very Ill at his Hands, that he should think himself Better in a Ditch, than in a Palace, and so he pass'd this Judgment upon him; that since he would not be persuaded to come out of his House upon that occasion, he should never Stir abroad again from that Day forward, without his House upon his Head.

THE MORAL. *There's a Retreat of Sloth and Affection, as well as of Choice and Virtue: and a Beggar may be as Proud, and as happy too in a Cottage, as a Prince in a Palace.*

ἀγανακτέω, be angry; + κατά τινος, be angry at/with someone or something

αἱρέω, take; (mid.) choose; + μᾶλλον ἤ, prefer to do X (inf.) more/rather than

αἰτία, ἡ, cause, reason

ἄλλος, -η, -ο, another

ἄνθρωπος, ὁ, man, person, human being

ἄριστος, -η, -ον, best

αὐτός, -ή, -ό, (pron. in gen., dat., acc.) him, her, it; them

βαστάζω, carry

γάμος, ὁ, (sing./pl.) marriage

δεῖπνον, τό, dinner

δηλόω, show, reveal

διαπορέω, be perplexed, be very confused, wonder (at)

ἑαυτοῦ, -ῆς, -οῦ (reflex. pron. in gen., dat., acc.), himself, herself, itself; themselves

ἐπί (prep. + acc.), to

ἑστιάω, throw a feast for, entertain; receive X (acc.) as guest(s) in one's house

ζάω/ζῶ, ζῆν (pres. inf.), live

Ζεύς, Διός, Διΐ, Δία, ὁ, Zeus

ζῷον/ζῶον, τό, animal, creature

ἤ (conj., w/ comp.), than

λέγω, λέξω/ἐρῶ, εἶπον, say

κατά (prep. + gen.), at or against (in a hostile sense)

καταδικάζω, condemn a person (gen.) to do X (inf.)

λιτῶς (adv.), plainly, simply

μᾶλλον (adv.), more

μονός, -ή, -όν, alone, only

μῦθος, ὁ, story, fable, tale

οἶκος, ὁ, house

ὅτι (conj.), that

παρά (prep. + dat.), in/at X's house(s)

παραγί(γ)νομαι, -γενήσομαι, παρεγενόμην, come to

πᾶς, πᾶσα, πᾶν, all, every

περιφέρω, carry around, carry about (with one); wander about

πολύς, πολλή, πολύ, much; (pl.) many; οἱ πολλοί, the majority, the common people

πολυτελῶς (adv.), lavishly

πυνθάνομαι, πεύσομαι, ἐπυθόμην, inquire of, ask (+ gen.)

τελέω, fulfill, accomplish; + γάμον/ γάμους, get married, celebrate one's wedding

τίς, τί (gen. τίνος; interrog. pron. and adj.), who? which? what?

ὑστερέω, come (too) late; be absent

ὑστέρησις, -εως, ἡ, being late, lateness; absence

φίλος, -η, -ον, dear, beloved

χάριν (prep. + gen.), for the sake of, on behalf of, on account of; + τίνος, for what reason?, why?

χελώνη, ἡ, tortoise

Dutch Woodcut (1727)

35

10. The Two Frogs
(Chambry 67/67 = Perry 69)

Δύο βάτραχοι ἀλλήλοις ἐγειτνίων. Ἐνέμοντο δὲ ὁ μὲν βαθείαν καὶ τῆς ὁδοῦ πόρρω λίμνην, ὁ δὲ ἐν ὁδῷ μικρὸν ὕδωρ ἔχων. Καὶ δὴ τοῦ ἐν τῇ λίμνῃ παραινοῦντος θατέρῳ μεταβῆναι πρὸς αὑτόν, ἵνα καὶ ἀμείνονος καὶ ἀσφαλεστέρας
5 διαίτης μεταλάβῃ, ἐκεῖνος οὐκ ἐπείθετο λέγων δυσαποσπάστως ἔχειν τῆς τοῦ τόπου συνηθείας, ἕως οὗ συνέβη ἅμαξαν τῇδε παριοῦσαν θλᾶσαι αὐτόν.

Οὕτω καὶ τῶν ἀνθρώπων οἱ τοῖς φαύλοις ἐπιτηδεύμασιν ἐνδιατρίβοντες φθάνουσιν ἀπολλύμενοι πρὶν ἢ ἐπὶ τὰ
10 καλλίονα τρέπεσθαι.

1-3 Ἐνέμοντο...ἔχων ἔχων is redundant after Ἐνέμοντο, but does create a sort of chiasmus: Ἐνέμοντο (A) ὁ μὲν (B), ὁ δὲ (B) ἔχων (A)

1-2 ὁ μὲν...ὁ δὲ 'the one...the other...'

3 τοῦ...παραινοῦντος gen. abs.
θατέρῳ = Attic contraction of τῷ + ἑτέρῳ

6 δυσαποσπάστως ἔχειν indir. disc. governed by λέγων. Gk. ἔχω + adv. = English εἰμί + adj. (Smyth § 1438)
τῆς τοῦ τόπου συνηθείας gen. of separation (Smyth § 1392)

9 φθάνουσιν ἀπολλύμενοι 'are first ruined/destroyed'

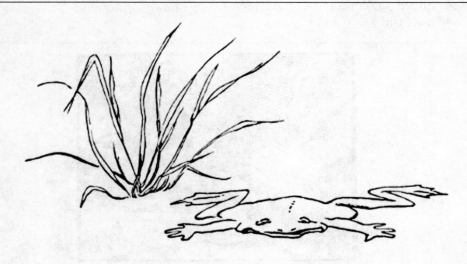

Randolph Caldecott (design), J. D. Cooper (engraving) (1883)

ἀλλήλων, one another
ἄμαξα, ἡ, wagon
ἀμείνων, -ον, -ονος (gen.), better
ἄνθρωπος, ὁ, man, person, human being
ἀπόλλυμι, destroy, ruin
ἀσφαλής, -ές, safe, safe from danger
αὐτός, -ή, -ό, (pron. in gen., dat., acc.)
   him, her, it; them
βαθύς, βαθεῖα, βαθύ, deep
βάτραχος, ὁ, frog
γειτνιάω, be a neighbor to (+ dat.)
δή (particle), in truth, indeed; καὶ δή,
   and what is more
δίαιτα, ἡ, way of living, mode of life;
   dwelling, abode
δύο (indecl.), two
δυσαποσπάστως (adv.), in a manner
   hard to tear oneself away
ἐκεῖνος, ἐκείνη, ἐκεῖνο, that; (pl.)
   those
ἐνδιατρίβω, continue doing X (dat.),
   waste time in doing X (dat.)
ἐπί (prep. + acc.), to
ἐπιτήδευμα, -ατος, pursuit
ἕτερος, -α, -ον, other, another;
   (usu. w/ article) the other (one of two)
ἔχω, have; dwell in, inhabit
ἕως (adv.), until; ἕως οὗ, until the time
   when
θλάω, crush
ἵνα (conj. + subju.), that, in order that
καλλίων, -ον, (-ονος, gen.), better,
   finer
λέγω, say
λίμνη, ἡ, pond, pool, lake

μεταβαίνω, μεταβήσομαι,
   μετέβην, go from one place to
   another
μεταλαμβάνω, μεταλήψομαι,
   μετέλαβον, have or get a share of
   X, share in one's X, share with one X
   (+ gen.)
μικρός, -ά, -όν, small, little, small
   amount of
νέμω, distribute; (mid.) dwell in,
   inhabit
ὁδός, ὁδοῦ, ἡ, road
ὅς, ἥ, ὅ (rel. pron.), who, whose,
   whom, which, that
οὕτω/οὕτως (adv.), so, thus, in
   this way
παραινέω, exhort, urge, advise
   (+ dat.)
πάρειμι, pass or go by, go past
πείθω, persuade; (mid./pass.) listen to
πόρρω (adv.), far from (+ gen.)
πρίν (adv.), + ἤ, before (+ inf.)
συμβαίνω, συμβήσομαι, συνέβην,
   (3rd sing. often impersonal) come
   to pass, happen (often + acc. and inf.)
συνήθεια, ἡ, customary or habitual
   usage of; being used to X (gen.)
τῇδε (adv.), here, in this place
τόπος, ὁ, place, spot
τρέπω, turn; (mid./pass) turn oneself
   (to)
ὕδωρ, ὕδατος, τό, water
φαῦλος, -η, -ον, trivial, worthless,
   thoughtless
φθάνω, (+ part., often translated into
   English as adv. 'first' while part. is
   translated as indic. vb.)

11. The Frogs Seek a King
(Chambry 66/66 = Perry 44)

Βάτραχοι λυπούμενοι ἐπὶ τῇ ἑαυτῶν ἀναρχίᾳ πρέσβεις
ἔπεμψαν πρὸς τὸν Δία, δεόμενοι βασιλέα αὐτοῖς παρασχεῖν.
Ὁ δὲ συνιδὼν τὴν εὐήθειαν αὐτῶν ξύλον εἰς τὴν λίμνην
καθῆκε. Καὶ οἱ βάτραχοι, τὸ μὲν πρῶτον καταπλαγέντες
5 τὸν ψόφον, εἰς τὰ βάθη τῆς λίμνης ἐνέδυσαν. Ὕστερον δὲ,
ὡς ἀκίνητον ἦν τὸ ξύλον, ἀναδύντες εἰς τοσοῦτον
καταφρονήσεως ἦλθον ὡς ἐπιβαίνοντες αὐτῷ ἐπι-
καθέζεσθαι. Ἀναξιοπαθοῦντες δὲ τοιοῦτον ἔχειν βασιλέα,
ἧκον ἐκ δευτέρου πρὸς τὸν Δία καὶ τοῦτον παρεκάλουν
10 ἀλλάξαι αὐτοῖς τὸν ἄρχοντα· τὸν γὰρ πρῶτον λίαν εἶναι
νωχελῆ. Καὶ ὁ Ζεὺς ἀγανακτήσας καθ' αὐτῶν ὕδρον αὐτοῖς
ἔπεμψεν, ὑφ' οὗ συλλαμβανόμενοι κατησθίοντο.

Ὁ λόγος δηλοῖ ὅτι ἄμεινόν ἐστι νωθεῖς καὶ μὴ πονηροὺς
ἔχειν ἄρχοντας ἢ ταρακτικοὺς καὶ κακούργους.

---

2 **δεόμενοι** sc. αὐτοῦ
4 **καταπλαγέντες** masc. nom. pl. aor. pass. part. < καταπλήσσω
6-7 **εἰς τοσοῦτον καταφρονήσεως ἦλθον** lit., 'they came into so much of
disdain/contempt (of it),' i.e., they became so disdainful/contemptuous (of it)
8 **Ἀναξιοπαθοῦντες δὲ τοιοῦτον ἔχειν βασιλέα** lit., 'and being
indignant at unworthy treatment that they were having such a (bad) king as
this,' i.e., and being deeply upset at having such a bad king as this who was
unworthy of them
10-11 **τὸν γὰρ πρῶτον λίαν εἶναι νωχελῆ** implied indir. disc.; sc. εἶπον

Arthur Rackham (1912)

ἀγανακτέω, be angry; + κατά τινος, be
   angry at/with someone
ἀκίνητος, -ον, motionless; inactive
ἀλλάσσω/ἀλλάττω, change, exchange
   X (acc.) for another
ἀμείνων, -ον, (-ονος, gen.), better
ἀναδύνω/ἀναδύω, ἀναδύσομαι,
   ἀνέδυν, come to the surface
ἀναξιοπαθέω, be indignant at unworthy
   treatment, be resentful over undeserved
   treatment
ἀναρχία, ἡ, lack of a leader,
   lawlessness, anarchy
ἄρχων, -οντος, ὁ, ruler
αὐτός, -ή, -ό, (pron. in gen., dat., acc.)
   him, her, it; them
βάθος, -εος, τό, depth, height; (pl.)
   depths, deep water
βασιλεύς, -έως, ὁ, king
βάτραχος, ὁ, frog
δέομαι, ask or beg X (gen.) to do Y (inf.)
δεύτερος, -α, -ον, second;
   ἐκ δευτέρου, for the second time, a
   second time
δηλόω, show, reveal
ἑαυτοῦ, -ῆς, -οῦ (reflex. pron. in gen.,
   dat., acc.), himself, herself, itself;
   themselves; his, her, its or their own
ἐνδύνω/ἐνδύω, ἐνδύσω ἐνέδυσα, go
   in, enter
ἐπί (prep. + dat.), at, by
ἐπιβαίνω, climb, climb up, climb up on
   (+ dat.)
ἐπικαθέζομαι, sit down on (+ dat.)
ἔρχομαι, ἐλεύσομαι, ἦλθον, come, go
εὐήθεια, ἡ, childlike simplicity, simple
   and unsophisticated nature
ἔχω, have
Ζεύς, Διός, Διΐ, Δία, ὁ, Zeus
ἤ (conj.; w/ comp.), than
ἥκω, have come; ἧκον, had come, came
καθίημι, καθήσω, καθῆκα, send down

κάκουργος, -ον, doing wrong,
   malicious, evil; damaging, harmful
κατά (prep. + gen.), at or against (in a
   hostile sense)
καταπλήσσω, terrify
καταφρόνησις, -εως, ἡ, contempt,
   disdain
κατεσθίω, eat up, devour
λίαν (adv.), exceedingly
λέγω, λέξω/ἐρῶ, εἶπον, say
λίμνη, ἡ, pond, pool, lake
λόγος, ὁ, story, tale
λυπέω, cause pain or grief, distress
νωθής, -ές, dull, stupid; lazy
νωχελής, -ές, dull; weak; lazy
ξύλον, τό, (single piece of) wood
ὅς, ἥ, ὅ (rel. pron.), who, whose,
   whom, which, that
ὅτι (conj.), that
οὗτος, αὕτη, τοῦτο, this; (pl.) these
παρακαλέω, call
παρέχω, παρέξω, παρέσχον, give,
   provide
πέμπω, send
πονηρός, -ά, -όν, wicked, bad
πρέσβυς, -εως/εος, ὁ, ambassador
πρῶτον/τὸ πρῶτον (adv.), at first
πρῶτος, -η, -ον, first
συλλαμβάνω, seize, grasp
συνεῖδον, (aor. only), observe;
   recognize
ταρακτικός, -ή, -όν, trouble-making
τοιοῦτος, -αύτη, -οῦτο, such as
   this; (frequently w/ implication based
   on context) so good/bad/etc. ...as this
τοσοῦτον (adv.), so great, so much
ὕδρος, ὁ, water-snake
ὑπό (prep. + gen.) (w/ pass. voice), by
ὕστερον (adv.), later, afterwards
ψόφος, ὁ, sound, noise
ὡς (conj.), since; (= ὥστε), so that,
   w/ the result that (+ inf.)

L'Estrange (1692)

In the days of old, when the *Frogs* were all at liberty in the Lakes, and grown quite weary of living without Government, they petition'd *Jupiter* for a *King*, to the end that there might be some Distinction of good and Evil, by certain equitable Rules and Methods of Reward and Punishment. *Jupiter*, that knew the Vanity of their Hearts, threw them down a *Log* for their Governor; which upon the first Dash, frighted the whole *Mobile* of them into the Mud for the very fear on't. This *Panick* Terror kept them in Awe for a while, till in good time one *Frog*, bolder than the rest, put up his Head, and look'd about him, to see how Squares went with their *New King*. Upon this, he calls his Fellow-Subjects together, opens the Truth of the Case, and nothing would serve them then, but riding a-top of him; insomuch that the Dread they were in before, is now turn'd into Insolence and Tumult. *This King*, they said, was too *tame* for them, and *Jupiter* must needs be entreated to send 'em another: He did so; but Authors are divided upon it, whether 'twas a *Stork* or a *Serpent*; though whether of the two soever it was, he left them neither Liberty nor Property, but made a Prey of his Subjects. Such was their Condition, in fine, that they sent *Mercury* to *Jupiter* yet once again for *another King*, whose Answer was this: *They that will not be contented when they are well, must be patient when things are amiss with them*; and People had better rest where they are, than go farther and fare worse.

THE MORAL. *The Mobile are uneasy without a Ruler: They are as restless with one; and oftner they shift, the worse they are: so that Government or no Government, a King of God's making or of the Peoples, or none at all, the Multitude are never to be satisfied.*

Linton (1887)

The Frogs prayed to Jove for a king:
Not a log, but a livelier thing.
Jove sent them a Stork,
Who did royal work,
For he gobbled them up, did their king.

DON'T HAVE KINGS

Jacobs (1894)

The Frogs were living as happy as could be in a marshy swamp that just suited them; they went splashing about caring for nobody and nobody troubling with them. But some of them thought that this was not right, that they should have a king and a proper constitution, so they determined to send up a petition to Jove to give them what they wanted. "Mighty Jove," they cried, "send unto us a king that will rule over us and keep us in order." Jove laughed at their croaking, and threw down into the swamp a huge Log, which came down - kerplash! - into the swamp. The Frogs were frightened out of their lives by the commotion made in their midst, and all rushed to the bank to look at the horrible monster; but after a time, seeing that it did not move, one or two of the boldest of them ventured out towards the Log, and even dared to touch it; still it did not move. Then the greatest hero of the Frogs jumped upon the Log and commenced dancing up and down upon it, thereupon all the Frogs came and did the same; and for some time the Frogs went about their business every day without taking the slightest notice of their new King Log lying in their midst. But this did not suit them, so they sent another petition to Jove, and said to him, "We want a real king; one that will really rule over us." Now this made Jove angry, so he sent among them a big Stork that soon set to work gobbling them all up. Then the Frogs repented when too late.

Better no rule than cruel rule.

Richard Heighway (1894)

41

La Fontaine (1668)
(trans. Hill [2008])

Weary of swamp democracy,
The frogs made a cacophony
So rude, so raucous, so anarchic,
That Jupiter to shush them made their state monarchic.
He dropped them down a king not in the least bit harsh,
But whose arrival caused such panic in the marsh
That all that popeyed population,
A cowardly and stupid nation,
Dived in the water, hid in the weeds,
Sank into holes, shrank among reeds,
Not daring just at first to face
This conquering king who came from some new giant race –
Though, actually, he was a toppled tree
Whose air of gravity caused awe initially,
Until at last one frog dared take a look and see.
Trembling, she emerged, then cautiously hopped near;
Another followed her, another in the rear,
And soon a mob had formed
That so forgot respect
That all together stormed
Their king and sat upon his shoulders, quite unchecked!
The king stayed calm and let the revolution run,
But Jupiter felt splitting pressure in his brain:
"Give us," yelled the frogs, "a king who gets things done!"
The monarch of the gods this time sent a crane
Who speared them, who crunched them
On arbitrary grounds.
And then the frogs made louder sounds.
So Jupiter spoke out, "What now? Am I to swerve
Your nation's laws to fit each new opinion poll?
The first concern you should have had was to preserve
Your government.
But having failed that, you should have been content
To live in the benevolent control
Of that sweet-natured figurehead I sent.

So now fall silent and accept your curse,
For fear you'll go from bad to worse!"

Richard Heighway (1894)

43

Celia M. Fiennes (1926)

Arthur Rackham (1912)

Frederick Burr Opper (1916)

Anonymous (1916)[8]

In the lakes and ponds throughout the world the Frogs led a free and easy life. They came together, however, in a convention and petitioned Jupiter to let them have a King who would inspect their morals and make them live more honestly.

Jupiter, being in a good humor, laughed heartily at their request, and throwing a log down into the pool, cried, "There is a King for you!"

The sudden splash made by the fall at first so terrified the Frogs that they were afraid to approach their new King. Little by little, seeing it lay still, they ventured to come near it. At last, finding there was no danger, they leapt upon it and treated it as familiarly as they pleased.

Frederick Burr Opper (1916)

---

[8] From *Aesop's Fables with 100 Illustrations by F. Opper* (Philadelphia: J. B. Lippincott Company, 1916).

They soon became discontented with such a do-nothing King and they sent their deputies to ask for another sort. Upon that Jupiter sent them a Stork, who, without any ceremony, began to gobble them up as fast as he could. They then begged Mercury to tell Jupiter that they earnestly wanted to have another King, or to be left in the state in which they originally were.

Frederick Burr Opper (1916)

"No," says Jupiter, "let the obstinate wretches suffer the punishment due the foolishness of their choice."

MORAL: Frogs and people who want kings deserve whatever evils happen *to them*.

Frederick Burr Opper (1916)

47

12. The Gnat and the Lion
(Chambry 189/188 = Perry 255)

Κώνωψ πρὸς λέοντα ἐλθὼν εἶπεν· "Οὔτε φοβοῦμαί σε,
οὔτε δυνατώτερός μου εἶ· εἰ δὲ μή, τί σοί ἐστιν ἡ δύναμις;
ὅτι ξύεις τοῖς ὄνυξι καὶ δάκνεις τοῖς ὀδοῦσι; τοῦτο καὶ γυνὴ
τῷ ἀνδρὶ μαχομένη ποιεῖ. Ἐγὼ δὲ λίαν ὑπάρχω σου
5   ἰσχυρότερος. Εἰ δὲ θέλεις, ἔλθωμεν καὶ εἰς πόλεμον." Καὶ
σαλπίσας ὁ κώνωψ ἐνεπήγετο, δάκνων τὰ περὶ τὰς ῥίνας
αὐτοῦ ἄτριχα πρόσωπα. Καὶ ὁ λέων τοῖς ἰδίοις ὄνυξι
κατέλυεν ἑαυτόν, ἕως ἀπηύδησεν. Ὁ δὲ κώνωψ νικήσας τὸν
λέοντα, σαλπίσας καὶ ἐπινίκιον ᾄσας, ἔπτατο· καὶ ἀράχνης
10 δεσμῷ ἐμπλακεὶς ἐσθιόμενος ἀπωδύρετο πῶς μεγίστοις
πολεμῶν ὑπό εὐτελοῦς ζώου, τῆς ἀράχνης, ἀπώλετο.

---

2   *μου* gen. of comparison (Smyth § 1069) So too *σου* in l. 4, even though
there the pron. precedes its comp. adj. rather than, as in English idiom,
follows it
εἰ δὲ μή lit., 'but if not,' i.e., but if you don't believe that/think otherwise
3   *τοῖς ὄνυξι...δάκνεις τοῖς ὀδοῦσι* instrumental datives (Smyth § 1507)
5   *ἔλθωμεν* 1st pl. aor. act. subju. < *ἔρχομαι*; hortatory subju.
5-6 *εἰς πόλεμον...σαλπίσας* the language is that of a military campaign.
Trumpets (*ἡ σάλπιγξ*) were primarily employed before battle to summon
one's troops and to sound the charge
10   *δεσμῷ* instrumental dat. (Smyth § 1507)
ἐμπλακεὶς masc. nom. sing. aor. pass. part. < *ἐμπλέκω*
μεγίστοις sc. *ζώοις*
11   *τῆς ἀράχνης* in apposition to *εὐτελοῦς ζώου*

Alexander Calder (1931)

ἀείδω, ᾁσομαι, ᾖσα, sing
ἀνήρ, ἀνδρός, ὁ, man, husband
ἀπαυδάω, become out of breath, faint;
   refuse (to fight more), cry 'uncle'
ἀποδύρομαι, lament bitterly
ἀπολλύμι, ἀπολέσω/ἀπολῶ,
   ἀπώλεσα, destroy, kill
ἀράχνη, ἡ, spider's web; spider
ἄτριχος, -ον, without hair
αὐτός, -ή, -ό, (pron. in gen., dat.,
   acc.) him, her, it; them
γυνή, -αικός, ἡ, woman, wife
δάκνω, bite, sting
δεσμός, ὁ, bonds, imprisonment
δύναμις, -εως, ἡ, power
δυνατός, -ή, -όν, strong, powerful
ἑαυτοῦ, ἑαυτῆς, ἑαυτοῦ, (refl. pron.
   in gen., dat., acc.) himself, herself,
   itself
ἐμπλέκω, entwine, entangle
ἐνεπάγομαι, (mid. only) attack
ἐπινίκιον, τό, song of victory
ἔρχομαι, ἐλεύσομαι, ἦλθον, go,
   come
ἐσθίω, eat
εὐτελής, -ές, worthless, insignificant
ἕως (adv.), until
ζῷον/ζῶον, τό, animal, creature,
   living being
θέλω/ἐθέλω, be willing (+ inf.)

ἴδιος, -α, -ον, one's own
ἰσχυρός, -ά, -όν, strong, powerful
καταλύω, destroy
κώνωψ, -ωπος, ὁ, gnat
λέγω, λέξω/ἐρῶ, εἶπον, say
λέων, -οντος, ὁ, lion
λίαν (adv.), very much
μάχομαι, fight with (+ dat.)
μέγας, μεγάλη, μέγα, great, mighty
νικάω, defeat, conquer, vanquish (+ acc.)
ξύω, scratch
ὀδούς, -όντος, ὁ, tooth
ὄνυξ, -υχος, ὁ, nail, claw
ὅτι (conj.), that, the fact that
οὔτε, and not, not, nor; οὔτε...οὔτε,
   neither...nor
οὗτος, αὕτη, τοῦτο, this; (pl.) these
πέτομαι, πετήσομαι, ἐπτάμην,
   fly, fly away
ποιέω, do
πολεμέω, fight, do battle w/ (+ dat.)
πόλεμος, ὁ, battle, fight; war
πρόσωπον, τό, (mostly in pl., even
   of a single person) face
πῶς (adv.), how?
ῥίς, ῥινός, ἡ, nose; (pl.) nostrils, nose
σαλπίζω, sound the trumpet
ὑπάρχω (= εἰμί), be
ὑπό, (prep. + gen.) (w/ pass. voice) by
φοβέομαι/φοβοῦμαι, be afraid, fear

Arthur Rackham (1912)

L'Estrange (1692)

As a *Lion* was Blustering in the Forrest, up comes a *Gnat* to his very Beard, and enters into an Expostulation with him upon the Points of Honour and Courage. What do I Value your Teeth or your Claws, says the *Gnat*, that are but the Arms of every Bedlam Slut? As to the Matter of Resolution; I defy ye to put that Point immediately to an Issue. So the Trumpet Sounded, and the Combatants enter'd the Lists. The *Gnat* charg'd into the Nostrils of the *Lion*, and there Twing'd him, till he made him Tear himself with his own Paws, and in the Conclusion he Master'd the *Lion*. Upon this, a Retreat was Sounded, and the *Gnat* flew his way: but by Ill-hap afterward, in his Flight, he struck into a Cobweb, where the *Victor* fell Prey to a *Spider*. This Disgrace went to the Heart of him, after he had got the Better of a *Lion*, to be Worsted by an *Insect*.

THE MORAL. *'Tis the Power of Fortune to Humble the Pride of the Mighty, even by the most Despicable Means, and to make a Gnat Triumph over a Lion: Wherefore let no Creature, how Great or Little soever, Presume on the One side, or Despair on the Other.*

Goldsmith (1784)

Little minds are so much elevated by any advantage gained over their superiors, that they are often thrown off their guard against a sudden change of fortune.

Avaunt! thou paltry contemptible insect! said a proud Lion one day to a Gnat that was frisking about in the air near his den. The Gnat, enraged at this unprovoked insult, vowed revenge, and immediately darted into the Lion's ear. After having sufficiently teased him in that quarter, she quitted her station and retired under his belly, and from thence made her last and most formidable attack in his nostrils, where stinging him almost to madness, the Lion at length fell down, utterly spent with rage, vexation, and pain. The Gnat having thus abundantly gratified her resentment, flew off in great exultation; but in the heedless transports of her success, not sufficiently attending to her own security, she found herself unexpectedly entangled in the web of a spider; who, rushing out instantly upon her, put an end to her triumph and her life.

This fable instructs us, never to suffer success so far to transport us as to throw us off our guard against a reverse of fortune.

La Fontaine (1668)
(Hill [2008])

"Begone, ignoble insect! Speck of excrement!"
The lion one day told the gnat,
Or roared to this effect, whereat
The gnat immediately went
To war. "King, sweetie, thinkest thou
Your royal title makes me get cold feet?
A mean old bull is twice as strong as you
And I make him do any tricks I want him to,
So when I see you, baby, all I see is meat!"
No sooner was this spoken than
With his small trumpet he began
To sound the charge, this one-gnat band
And street guerilla both combined.
He mobilised, struck tail and mane,
And drove the lion near insane.
The quadruped began to froth, his eyes glowed red.
He roared! Small creatures hid and great ones fled:
A scene of universal dread
Accomplished by one tiny gnat.
This dwarfish fly zoomed all about,
He stung the lion's rump, he stung the lion's snout,
Then flew inside of that and stung.
The lion's mounting fury reached its topmost rung:
His unseen foe was winning, gleeful as it saw
How in his rampant fury every tooth and claw
Performed the butcher's job for which it was designed –
The lion bled from many a self-inflicted wound.
He lashed his tail along his flanks,
But only struck thin air; his mane fell out of hanks,
Until frustrated rage so weakened him he swooned!
The insect left the field with oak leaves on his brow;
As earlier the charge, he sounded victory now!
But soon thereafter, going through the world to tell
His glorious feat, proceeding down a road he fell
Into a spider's ambush – and met his end as well.
Is there perhaps a lesson to be drawn from this?
Well, I see two. The first: if one has enemies
The ones to fear the most are often least in size.
And, second: one may come through holocausts untouched
Then choke upon a grain of rice.

13. The Deer and the Vine
(Chambry 104 = Perry 77)

Ἔλαφος διωκομένη ὑπὸ κυνηγῶν ἐκρύπτετο ὑπό τινα
ἄμπελον. Διελθόντων δὲ τῶν κυνηγῶν, στραφεῖσα κατήσθιε
τὰ φύλλα τῆς ἀμπέλου. Εἷς δέ τις τῶν κυνηγῶν στραφεὶς καὶ
θεασάμενος, ὃ εἶχεν ἀκόντιον βαλών, ἔτρωσεν αὐτήν. Ἡ δὲ
5   μέλλουσα τελευτᾶν στενάξασα πρὸς ἑαυτὴν ἔφη· "Δίκαιά γε
πάσχω, ὅτι τὴν σώσασάν με ἄμπελον ἠδίκησα."

Οὗτος ὁ λόγος λεχθείη ἂν κατὰ ἀνδρῶν οἵτινες τοὺς
εὐεργέτας ἀδικοῦντες ὑπὸ θεοῦ κολάζονται.

---

2   Διελθόντων...τῶν κυνηγῶν gen. abs.
      στραφεῖσα fem. nom. sing. aor. pass. part. < στρέφω
4   ὃ εἶχεν ἀκόντιον βαλών = βαλών ἀκόντιον ὃ εἶχεν
6   ἄμπελον in apposition to τὴν σώσασάν με
7   λόγος λεχθείη rhetorical trope known as *figura etymologica*, in which
      a vb. governs its related noun
      λεχθείη 3rd sing. aor. pass. opt. < λέγω; potential opt. (Smyth § 1824)

L'Estrange (1692)

A *Goat* that was hard Press'd by the Huntsmen, took Sanctuary in a
Vineyard, and there he lay Close, under the covert of a *Vine*. So soon as
he thought the Danger was Over, he fell presently to Browzing upon the
Leaves; and whether it was the Rusling, or the Motion of the Boughs,
that gave the Huntsmen an Occasion for stricter Search, is Uncertain:
But a Search there was, and in the End he was Discover'd and Shot. He
dy'd, in fine, with this Conviction upon him, that his Punishment was
Just, for Offering Violence to his Protector.

THE MORAL. *Ingratitude Perverts all the Measures of Religion and Society,
by making it Dangerous to be Charitable and Good Natur'd.*

ἀδικέω, injure, do wrong to

ἀκόντιον, τό, javelin

ἄμπελος, ἡ, vine, grape-vine

ἀνήρ, ἀνδρός, ὁ, man

αὐτός, -ή, -ό, (pron. in gen., dat., acc.) him, her, it; them

γε (enclitic particle, giving emphasis to the word or words which it follows. With single words, 'at least,' 'at any rate,' but often only to be rendered by italics in writing, or emphasis in pronunciation)

διέρχομαι, διελεύσομαι/δίειμι, διῆλθον, pass by

δίκαιος, -α, -ον, right, just; (neut. pl. w/ adverbial force)

διώκω, pursue, chase, hunt

ἑαυτοῦ, -ῆς, -οῦ (reflex. pron. in gen., dat., acc.), himself, herself, itself; themselves

εἷς, μία, ἕν one

ἔλαφος, ὁ/ἡ, deer

εὐεργέτης, -ου, ὁ, benefactor

ἔχω, have

θεάομαι, see, see clearly

θεός, ὁ, god

κατά (prep. + gen.), against (in a hostile sense)

κατεσθίω, eat up, devour

κολάζω, punish

κρύπτω, hide, conceal

κυνηγός, ὁ, hunter

λέγω, say

λόγος, ὁ, tale, story

μέλλω, be about to (+ fut. inf.)

ὅς, ἥ, ὅ (rel. pron.), who, whose, whom, which, that

ὅστις, ἥτις, ὅ τι, anyone who, anything which

ὅτι (causal particle), because

οὗτος, αὕτη, τοῦτο, this; (pl.) these

πάσχω, suffer

στενάζω, στενάξω, ἐστέναξα, groan

στρέφω, turn; (mid./pass.) turn oneself, turn around or about

σῴζω, save (from death), keep alive

τελευτάω, die

τις, τι, (gen. τινος) (indef. adj.) a certain; some; a, an

τιτρώσκω, τρώσω, ἔτρωσα, wound

ὑπό (prep. + gen.), (w/ pass. voice) by; (+ acc.) under

φημί, φήσω, ἔφην, say

φύλλον, -ου, τό, leaf

Linton (1887)

A Hart by the hunters pursued,
Safely hid in a Vine, till he chewed
The sweet tender green,
And, through shaking leaves seen,
He was slain by his ingratitude.

SPARE YOUR BENEFACTORS

14. The Fir Tree and the Bramble Bush
(Babrius 64 = Perry 304)

Ἤριζον ἐλάτη καὶ βάτος πρὸς ἀλλήλας.

ἐλάτης δ' ἑαυτὴν πολλαχῶς ἐπαινούσης·

"καλὴ μέν εἰμι καὶ τὸ μέτρον εὐμήκης,

καὶ τῶν νεφῶν σύνοικος ὀρθίη φύω,

5   στέγης τε μέλαθρον εἰμι καὶ τρόπις πλοίων·

δένδρῳ τοσούτῳ πῶς, ἄκανθα, συγκρίνῃ;"

βάτος πρὸς αὐτὴν εἶπεν "ἢν λάβῃς μνήμην

τῶν πελέκεών τε τῶν ἀεί σε κοπτόντων,

βάτος γενέσθαι καὶ σὺ μᾶλλον αἱρήσῃ."

10   Ἅπας ὁ λαμπρὸς τῶν ἐλαττόνων μᾶλλον

καὶ δόξαν ἔσχε χὑπέμεινε κινδύνους.

---

2   ἐλάτης...ἐπαινούσης gen. abs.

3   τὸ μέτρον acc. of respect (Smyth § 1600)

6   ἄκανθα voc.
      συγκρίνῃ 2nd sing. pres. mid./pass. indic or 2nd fut. mid. < συγκρίνω

7   ἢν λάβῃς...αἱρήσῃ FMV condit.
      ἤν (= εἰ + ἄν), if (ever) (+ subju.)

8   Note alliteration, 'driving' home the bramble bush's 'point'

10   τῶν ἐλαττόνων gen. of comparison (Smyth § 1068, 1069). Note that in Gk.
      the comp. (μᾶλλον...δόξαν) can *follow* a gen. of comparison
      μᾶλλον governs both δόξαν and κινδύνους

11   ἔσχε χὑπέμεινε gnomic aorists (Smyth § 1931); translate as pres.
      χὑπέμεινε = καὶ + ὑπέμεινε

ἀεί (adv.), always

αἱρέω, take; (mid.) choose; + μᾶλλον, prefer to do/be X (inf.)

ἄκανθα, -ης, ἡ, thorn; prickly plant

ἀλλήλων, one another

ἅπας, ἅπασα, ἅπαν, all, every

αὐτός, -ή, -ό, (adj.) -self, -selves; (pron. in gen., dat., acc.) him, her, it, them

βάτος, ἡ, bramble bush, wild raspberry

γί(γ)νομαι, γενήσομαι, ἐγενόμην, be

δένδρον, τό, tree

δόξα, ἡ, glory, reputation, fame

ἑαυτοῦ, -ῆς, -οῦ, of himself, herself, itself

ἐλάσσων/ἐλάττων, -ον (gen. -ονος), smaller; (of people) lesser

ἐλάτη, ἡ, fir tree

ἐπαινέω, praise, sing X's (acc.) praises

ἐρίζω, quarrel

εὐμήκης, -ες, tall, great

ἔχω, ἕξω, ἔσχον, have

καλός, -ή, -όν, beautiful

κίνδυνος, ὁ, danger

κόπτω, strike, chop, fell (trees)

λαμβάνω, λήψομαι, ἔλαβον, take; + μνήμην, recall, call to mind, remember (+ gen.)

λαμπρός, -ή, -όν, famous, distinguished

λέγω, λέξω/ἐρῶ, εἶπον, say

μᾶλλον (adv.), more

μέλαθρον, τό, the main beam which bears the ceiling; roof

μέτρον, τό, size

μνήμη, ἡ, memory, remembrance of (+ gen.)

νέφος, -εος, τό, cloud

ὄρθιος, -η, -ον, straight up, upright

πέλεκυς, -εως, ὁ, ax/axe

πλοῖον, τό, ship

πολλαχῶς (adv.), in many ways

πῶς, how? (sometimes to express displeasure) how is it that?

στέγη, ἡ, roof; house

σύ, σοῦ/σου, σοί/σοι, σέ/σε, you

συγκρίνω, compare; (mid.) compare oneself w/ another (dat.)

σύνοικος, -ον, dwelling in the same house w/, fellow inhabitant of (+ gen.)

τε (particle), in later verse, often not easily translatable; perhaps here giving an epic 'coloring' or 'elevation' to the bramble bush's reproach

τοσοῦτος, -αύτη, -οῦτο, so large, so tall, so great

τρόπις, ἡ, ship's keel

ὑπομένω, ὑπομενῶ, ὑπέμεινα, undergo, endure

φύω, grow

Linton (1887)

The Fir-tree looked down on the Bramble.
"Poor thing only able to scramble
About on the ground."
Just then an axe' sound
Made the Fir wish himself but a Bramble.

PRIDE OF PLACE HAS ITS DISADVANTAGES

15. The Shepherd and the Wolf Cubs
(Chambry 314 [Variant 2] = Perry 209)

Ποιμὴν εὑρὼν λυκίδια, ἔτρεφεν ἐπιμελῶς, οἰόμενος ὅτι
μεγαλυνθέντα τηρήσουσι τὰ ἑαυτοῦ πρόβατα, ἀλλὰ καὶ ἔτι
προσθήσουσιν ἁρπάζοντες ἕτερα καὶ εἰσάξουσιν ἐν τῇ αὐτοῦ
μάνδρᾳ. Οἱ δέ, ὡς ηὐξήθησαν, πρῶτον αὐτοῦ τὴν ποίμνη
5 διέφθειραν. Καὶ ὃς ἀναστενάξας εἶπεν· "Δίκαια πέπονθα· τί γὰρ
μὴ νηπίους ἀπέκτεινον;"

Ὁ μῦθος δηλοῖ ὅτι οἱ τοὺς πονηροὺς διασώζοντες
λανθάνουσι καθ' ἑαυτῶν πρῶτον αὐτοὺς ῥωννύντες.

---

2 μεγαλυνθέντα neut. nom. pl. aor. pass. part. < μεγαλύνω; i.e., after they
had grown up
μεγαλυνθέντα τηρήσουσι neut. pl. subj. ([λυκίδια] μεγαλυνθέντα) w/
pl. vb. "may be used when stress is laid on the fact that the neuter plural
subject is composed of persons or of several parts." (Smyth § 959). Here,
though, there does not seem to be such a stress, so perhaps this is simply a
somewhat rare L. Gk./Koine Gk. usage (see also the grammatical anomalies,
at least with reference to 'strict' Cl. Gk. norms, pointed out in notes **3** and **3-4**)

3 προσθήσουσιν sc. τὰ ἑαυτοῦ πρόβατα
ἁρπάζοντες note (ungrammatical) shift from neut. nom. pl. part.
(μεγαλυνθέντα) to masc. nom. pl., perhaps because now they are viewed as
grown-up λύκοι
ἕτερα sc. πρόβατα

3-4 ἐν τῇ αὐτοῦ μάνδρᾳ = (Cl. Gk.) εἰς τὴν ἑαυτοῦ μάνδραν

4 ηὐξήθησαν 3rd pl. aor. pass. indic. < αὐξάνω

5 καὶ ὅς 'and he', occurs at the beginning of a clause in post-Homeric Gk.
(in Homeric Greek ὅς, ἥ, ὅ were originally demonstrative pronouns)
πέπονθα 3rd sing. perf. act. indic. < πάσχω

6 μὴ Cl. Gk. would use οὐ

7-8 λανθάνουσι...ῥωννύντες w/ λανθάνω + part., one usually translates the
part. as an indic. vb. (i.e., 'they are strengthening/making strong and mighty')
and λανθάνω as an adv. w/ the meaning 'unawares,' 'without noticing/
realizing it'

ἀναστενάζω, groan, lament

ἀποκτείνω, ἀποκτενῶ, ἀπέκτεινα, kill

ἁρπάζω, snatch away, carry off, plunder

αὐξάνω, increase; (pass.) grow up

αὐτός, -ή, -ό, (pron. in gen., dat., acc.) him, her, it; them

γάρ (particle), for (introduces the reason or cause of what precedes); τί γὰρ, why? (used in abrupt questions)

δηλόω, show, reveal

διασῴζω/διασώζω, preserve (through a danger), save

διαφθείρω, διαφθερῶ, διέφθειρα, destroy (utterly), kill

δίκαιος, -α, -ον, right, just; (neut. pl. with adverbial force)

ἑαυτοῦ, -ῆς, -οῦ, of himself, herself, itself; of his own, her own, its own

εἰσάγω, lead in/into

ἐπιμελῶς (adv.), w/ care and attention

ἕτερος, -η, -ον, another

ἔτι (adv.), besides, further, moreover

εὑρίσκω, εὑρήσω, εὗρον/ηὗρον, find

κατά (prep. + gen.), against (in a hostile sense)

λανθάνω, escape notice (+ part.)

λέγω, λέξω/ἐρῶ, εἶπον, say

λυκίδιον, τό, wolf cub

μάνδρα, ἡ, sheepfold

μεγαλύνω, make big

μῦθος, ὁ, story, fable, tale

νήπιος, ὁ, infant; young (of an animal)

οἴομαι, think

ὅς, ἥ, ὅ (rel. pron.), who, whose, whom, which, that

ὅτι (conj.), that

πάσχω, suffer

ποιμήν, -ένος, ὁ, shepherd

ποίμνη, ἡ, flock

πονηρός, -ά, -όν, wicked, bad

πρόβατον, -ου, τό, anything that walks [βαίνω] forward [πρό]; (mostly in pl.) generally of cattle, flocks, herds, sheep, goats

προστίθημι, προσθήσω, προσέθηκα, add to, augment

πρῶτον (adv.), first, in the first place; first of all, above all else

ῥώννυμι, strengthen, make strong and mighty

τηρέω, ὁ, guard, protect

τίς, τί (gen. τίνος; interrog. pron. and adj.), who? which? what?; ?; τί, 'why'?

τρέφω, (of slaves, cattle, dogs, etc.) rear and keep; feed

ὡς (conj. + indic. past tense vb.), when

16. The Wolf, the Dog, and the Collar
(Babrius 100 = Perry 346)

Λύκῳ συνήντα πιμελὴς κύων λίην.

ὁ δ' αὐτὸν ἐξήταζε, ποῦ τραφεὶς οὕτως

μέγας κύων ἐγένετο καὶ λίπους πλήρης.

"ἄνθρωπος" εἶπε "δαψιλής με σιτεύει."

5   "ὁ δέ σοι τράχηλος" εἶπε "πῶς ἐλευκώθη;"

"κλοιῷ τέτριπται σάρκα τῷ σιδηρείῳ,

ὃν ὁ τροφεύς μοι περιτέθεικε χαλκεύσας."

λύκος δ' ἐπ' αὐτῷ καγχάσας "ἐγὼ τοίνυν

χαίρειν κελεύω" φησί "τῇ τρυφῇ ταύτῃ,

10   δι' ἣν σίδηρος τὸν ἐμὸν αὐχένα τρίψει."

---

2   τραφεὶς masc. nom. sing. aor. pass. part. < τρέφω

5   σοι dat. of possession (Smyth §); so too μοι in l. 7
      ἐλευκώθη 3rd sing. aor. pass. indic. < λευκόω

6   κλοιῷ...τῷ σιδηρείῳ instrumental dat. (Smyth § 1503)
      τέτριπται 3rd sing. perf. mid./pass. indic. < τρίβω
      σάρκα acc. of respect (Smyth § 1600, 1601a)

7   χαλκεύσας masc. nom. sing. aor. act. part. < χαλκεύω
      περιτέθεικε 3rd sing. perf. act. indic. < περιτίθημι; sc. 'my neck' as dir. obj.

9   ταύτῃ οὗτος, αὕτη, τοῦτο often used emphatically, w/ an element of
      contempt

Randolph Caldecott (design), J. D. Cooper (engraving) (1883)

ἄνθρωπος, ὁ, man, person

αὐτός, -ή, -ό, (pron. in gen., dat., acc) him, her, it; them

αὐχήν, -ένος, ὁ, neck, throat

γί(γ)νομαι, ἐγενόμην (aor.), become

δαψιλής, -ές, generous

διά (prep. + gen.), through, by

ἐμός, -ή, -όν, my

ἐξετάζω, question (a person) closely

καγχάζω/καχάζω, laugh aloud, jeer, (+ ἐπί τινι, at one)

κλοιός, ὁ, dog-collar

κύων, κυνός, ὁ/ἡ, dog

λέγω, λέξω/ἐρῶ, εἶπον, say

λευκόω, whiten; bare; (pass.) be made or become white; become bare

λίαν/λίην (adv.), very, exceedingly

λίπος, -εος/ους, τό, (animal) fat

λύκος, ὁ, wolf

μέγας, μεγάλη, μέγα, big

ὅς, ἥ, ὅ (rel. pron.), who, whose, whom, which, that

οὗτος, αὕτη, τοῦτο, this; (pl.) these

οὕτως (adv.), thus, in this way

περιτίθημι, place/put around, put on

πιμελής, -ές, fat

πλήρης, -ες, full of (+ gen.)

ποῦ (adv.), where?

πῶς, how? (sometimes to express displeasure) how is it that?

σάρξ, σαρκός, ἡ, flesh

σίδηρος, ὁ, iron; (iron) chain

σιτεύω, feed, fatten

συναντάω, meet, encounter (+ dat.)

τοίνυν (inferential particle), therefore

τράχηλος, ὁ, neck, throat

τρέφω, (of slaves, cattle, dogs, etc.) rear and keep; feed

τρίβω, rub, wear out

τροφεύς, ὁ, one who rears or feeds

τρυφή, ἡ, luxury, luxuriousness

φημί, φήσω, ἔφην, say

χαίρω, rejoice; χαίρειν κελεύω, I say/bid farewell/good-bye

χαλκεύω, forge

L'Estrange (1692)

There was a hagged Carrion of a *Wolf*, and a jolly sort of a genteel *Dog*, with good Flesh upon's Back, that fell into Company together upon the King's Highway. The *Wolf* was wonderfully pleas'd with his Companion, and as inquisitive to learn how he brought himself to that blessed State of Body. Why, says the *Dog*, I keep my Master's House from Thieves, and I have very good Meat, Drink, and Lodging for my Pains. Now if you'll go along with me, and do as I do, you may fare as I fare. The *Wolf* struck up the Bargain, and so away they trotted together: But as they were jogging on, the *Wolf* spy'd a bare Place about the *Dog's* Neck, where the Hair was worn off. Brother (says he) how comes this, I prithee? Oh, that's nothing, says the *Dog*, but the fretting of my *Collar* a little. Nay says t'other, if there be a *Collar* in the Case, I know better things than to sell my Liberty for a Crust.

THE MORAL. *We are so dazzl'd with Glare of a splendid Appearance, that we can hardly discern the Inconveniences that attend it. 'Tis a Comfort to have good Meat and Drink at Command, and warm Lodging: But he that sells his Freedom, for the cramming of his Gut, has but a hard Bargain of it.*

Goldsmith (1784)

A prowling Wolf, that scour'd the plains,
To ease his hunger's griping pains,
Ragged as courtier in disgrace,
Hide-bound, and lean, and out of case,
By chance a well-fed Dog espy'd,
And being kin, and near ally'd,
He civilly salutes the cur:
"How do you, Cuz? Your servant sir.
O happy friend! how gay thy mien!
How plump thy sides, how sleek thy skin!
Triumphant plenty shines all o'er,
And the fat melts at ev'ry pore!
While I, alas! decay'd and old,
With hunger pin'd, and stiff with cold,
With many a howl and hideous groan,
Tell the relentless woods my moan.
Pr'ythee (my happy friend!) impart
Thy wondrous, cunning, thriving art."
"Why, faith, I'll tell thee as a friend,
But first thy surly manners mend;
Be complaisant, obliging, kind,
And leave the Wolf for once behind."
    The Wolf, whose mouth began to water,
With joy and rapture gallop'd after,
When thus the Dog: "At bed and board,
I share the plenty of my lord;
From ev'ry guest I claim a fee,
Who court my lord by bribing me.
In mirth I revel all the day,
And many a game at romps I play:
I fetch and carry, leap o'er sticks,
With twenty such diverting tricks."
"'Tis pretty, faith," the Wolf reply'd,
And on his neck the collar spy'd:
He starts, and without more ado,
He bids the abject wretch adieu:
"Enjoy your dainties, friend; to me
The noblest feast is liberty:
The famish'd Wolf, upon these desert plains,
Is happier than a fawning cur in chains."

Anonymous (1857)[9]

There was a gaunt, ragged, gipsy of a Wolf who fell into company with a sleek jolly Dog belonging to the spaniel tribe, on the King's highway. The Wolf was wonderfully pleased with his companion, and was inquisitive to learn how he had brought himself to that commendable state of body.

"Why," said the Dog, "I keep my Master's house, and I have the best of meat, drink, and lodging for my pains; indeed, if you'll go along with me, and do as I do, you may fare as I fare."

The Wolf readily agreed, and so away they trotted together; but as they approached the house the Wolf caught sight of the Dog's curiously embroidered collar, from which a kind of gold chain hung down over the shoulder. "Brother," said he, "what is this I see?"

"Oh, that's nothing," says the Spaniel; "a mere social Badge to let the world know whose Dog I am."

"Indeed!" says the other. "If those be the conditions, good bye. Bare bones and independence, rather than cold chicken with a chain and dog-collar."

MORAL.

To the independent spirit, gold fetters are as galling as iron ones.

Jacobs (1894)

A gaunt Wolf was almost dead with hunger when he happened to meet a House-dog who was passing by. "Ah, Cousin," said the Dog. "I knew how it would be; your irregular life will soon be the ruin of you. Why do you not work steadily as I do, and get your food regularly given to you?"

"I would have no objection," said the Wolf, "if I could only get a place."

"I will easily arrange that for you," said the Dog; "come with me to my master and you shall share my work."

So the Wolf and the Dog went towards the town together. On the way there the Wolf noticed that the hair on a certain part of the Dog's neck was very much worn away, so he asked him how that had come about.

---

[9] From *The Fables of Aesop and Others Translated into Human Nature. Designed and Drawn on the Wood by Charles H. Bennett*. London: W. Kent & Co., 1857.

"Oh, it is nothing," said the Dog. "That is only the place where the collar is put on at night to keep me chained up; it chafes a bit, but one soon gets used to it."

"Is that all?" said the Wolf. "Then good-bye to you, Master Dog."

Better starve free than be a fat slave.

Charles H. Bennett (1857)

17. The Wild Ass, the Donkey, and the Driver
(Chambry 265/264 = Perry 183)

Ὄνος ἄγριος ὄνον ἥμερον θεασάμενος ἔν τινι εὐηλίῳ τόπῳ προσελθὼν ἐμακάριζεν αὐτὸν ἐπὶ τῇ εὐεξίᾳ τοῦ σώματος καὶ τῇ τῆς τροφῆς ἀπολαύσει. Ὕστερον δὲ ἰδὼν αὐτὸν ἀχθοφοροῦντα καὶ τὸν ὀνηλάτην ὀπίσω ἑπόμενον καὶ
5 ῥοπάλῳ παίοντα εἶπεν· "Ἀλλ' ἔγωγε οὐκέτι σε εὐδαιμονίζω· ὁρῶ γὰρ ὅτι οὐκ ἄνευ κακῶν μεγάλων τὴν ἀφθονίαν ἔχεις."

Οὕτως οὐκ ἔστι ζηλωτὰ τὰ μετὰ κινδύνων καὶ ταλαιπωριῶν περιγινόμενα κέρδη."

---

1   θεασάμενος masc. nom. sing. aor. mid. (dep.) part. < θεάομαι
2   προσελθὼν masc. nom. sing. aor. act. part. < προσέρχομαι
3   τῇ τῆς τροφῆς ἀπολαύσει note word order
    ἰδὼν masc. nom. sing. aor. act. part. < ὁράω/ὁρῶ
8-9   Οὕτως...κέρδη = οὐκ οὕτως ζηλωτὰ ἔστι τὰ κέρδη περιγινόμενα μετὰ κινδύνων καὶ ταλαιπωριῶν. Neut. pl. subj. w/ sing. vb. is common in Gk.

ἄγριος, -ον, wild
ἄνευ (prep. + gen.), without
ἀπόλαυσις, ἡ, advantage got from (+ gen.)
ἀφθονία, ἡ, prosperity, abundance
ἀχθοφορέω, bear burdens, be loaded
ἔγωγε, strengthened form of ἔγω
ἐπί (prep. + dat.), on
ἔπομαι, follow
εὐδαιμονίζω, call/consider happy
εὐεξία, ἡ, good health/condition
εὐήλιος, -ον, sunny
ζηλωτός, -ή, -όν, enviable
ἥμερος, -ον, tame
θεάομαι, see; gaze at; contemplate
κακός, -ή, -όν, bad; (as substantive) evil, trouble
κέρδος, -εος, τό, gain, profit
κίνδυνος, ὁ, danger
λέγω, λέξω/ἐρῶ, εἶπον, say
μακαρίζω, congratulate, praise
μέγας, μεγάλη, μέγα, great

μετά (prep. + gen.), accompanied by,
ὀνηλάτης, -ου, ὁ, donkey-driver
ὄνος, ὁ/ἡ, ass
ὀπίσω (adv.), behind
ὁράω/ὁρῶ, ὄψομαι, εἶδον, see
ὅτι (conj.), that
οὐκέτι (adv.), no longer
οὕτω/οὕτως (adv.), so
παίω, strike, beat
περιγίγνομαι/περιγίνομαι, be left over, remain
προσέρχομαι, -ῆλθον (aor.), come or go forward, come forward to speak
ῥόπαλον, τό, club, cudgel (used to beat donkeys/asses/mules)
σῶμα, σώματος, τό, body
ταλαιπωρία, ἡ, hardship, distress; bodily suffering or pain
τις, τι, (gen. τινος) (indef. adj.) a, an
τόπος, ὁ, place, spot
τροφή, ἡ, food, diet
ὕστερον (adv.), later, afterwards

L'Estrange (1692)

As a *Tame Ass* was Airing himself in a Pleasant Meadow, with a Coat and Carcase in very good Plight, up comes a *Wild* One to him from the next Wood, with this short Greeting. *Brother* (says he) *I Envy your Happiness*; and so he left him: It was his Hap some short time after this Encounter, to see his *Tame Brother* Groaning under an Unmerciful Pack, and a Fellow at his Heels Goading him forward. He rounds him in the Ear upon't, and Whispers him, *My Friend* (says he) *your Condition is not, I perceive, what I took it to be, for a Body may buy Gold too Dear: And I am not for Purchasing good Looks and Provender at this Rate.*

THE MORAL. *Betwixt Envy and Ingratitude, we make Our selves twice Miserable; out of an Opinion, First, that Our Neighbour has too Much; and, Secondly, that We our Selves have too Little.*

18. The Wild Ass and the Donkey
(Syntipas 30 = Perry 411)

Ὄναγρος ὄνον ἰδὼν βαρὺν γόμον ἐπαγόμενον, καὶ τὴν
δουλείαν αὐτῷ ἐπονειδίζων, ἔλεγεν "εὐτυχὴς ὄντως ἐγώ, ὅτι
ζῶν ἐλευθέρως καὶ διάγων ἀκόπως αὐτοσχέδιον καὶ τὴν
νομὴν ἐν τοῖς ὄρεσι κέκτημαι· σὺ δὲ δι' ἄλλου τρέφῃ, καὶ
5   δουλείαις καὶ πληγαῖς καθυποβάλλῃ διηνεκῶς." συνέβη
γοῦν αὐθωρὸν λέοντά τινα φανῆναι καὶ τῷ μὲν ὄνῳ μὴ
προσπελάσαι, ὡς συνόντος αὐτῷ τοῦ ὀνηλάτου, τῷ δὲ
ὀνάγρῳ, μεμονωμένῳ τυγχάνοντι, σφοδρῶς ἐπελθεῖν καὶ
αὐτὸν θέσθαι κατάβρωμα.
10   Οὗτος δηλοῖ ὡς οἱ ἀνυπότακτοι καὶ σκληροτράχηλοι, τῇ
αὐτοβουλίᾳ φερόμενοι καὶ βοηθείας τινὸς μὴ δεόμενοι,
αὐθωρὸν πτῶμα γίνονται.

---

1   **ἰδὼν** masc. nom. sing. aor. act. part. < ὁράω/ὁρῶ
2   **εὐτυχὴς ὄντως ἐγώ** sc. εἰμί
4   **κέκτημαι** 1st sing. perf. mid./pass. (dep.) indic. < κτάομαι
5   **δουλείαις** abstract nouns in pl. become concrete, often referring to "cases,
occasions, [or] manifestations of the idea expressed by the abstract
substantive." (Smyth § 1000) Note too how the pl. contributes to the
alliteration: κ‍αὶ δουλείαις κ‍αὶ πληγαῖς
συνέβη 3rd sing. aor. act. indic.; + acc. and inf. in indir. disc.
6   **φανῆναι** aor. pass. inf. < φαίνω
7   **ὡς συνόντος...τοῦ ὀνηλάτου** "ὡς often indicates the thought or
assertion of the subject of the principal verb or of some other person
prominent in the sentence. Here ὡς expresses a real intention...[and is thus]
often [used] with participles." (Smyth § 2996). ὡς + gen. abs. = 'because
of...' (Smyth § 2086d)
8   **μεμονωμένῳ** masc. dat. sing. perf. mid./pass. part. < μονόω
9   **θέσθαι** aor. mid./pass. inf. < τίθημι
10   **Οὗτος** = Οὗτος μῦθος/λόγος

ἀκόπως (adv.), free from troubles, easily

ἄλλος, -η, -ο, another

ἀνυπότακτος, -ον, independent; obstinate

αὐθωρόν (adv.), in that very hour; immediately, at once

αὐτοβουλία, ἡ, stubbornness-itself, one's own sense of stubbornness (Gibbs)

αὐτός, -ή, -ό, (pron. in gen., dat., acc.) him, her, it, them

αὐτοσχέδιος, -ον, near at hand

βαρύς, -εῖα, -ύ, heavy

βοηθεία, ἡ, help, assistance

γί(γ)νομαι, become

γόμος, ὁ, (beast's) load

γοῦν (particle), οὖν ('then') + γε (putting emphasis on the word that precedes it)

δέομαι (dep.), ask X (gen.) for Y (gen.)

δηλόω, show, reveal

διά (prep. + gen.), through, by

διάγω, spend one's life, live

διηνεκῶς (adv.), continuously

δουλεία, ἡ, slavery, enslavement

ἐλευθέρως (adv.), freely

ἐπάγω, bring on; (mid.) bring w/ one

ἐπέρχομαι, -ῆλθον (aor.), attack

ἐπονειδίζω, insult/reproach X (dat.) for Y (acc.), cast X (acc.) in Y's (dat.) teeth

εὐτυχής, -ές, lucky, fortunate

ζῶ, live

καθυποβάλλω, place under; subject; (mid./pass.) subject oneself to/be subjected to (+ dat.)

κατάβρωμα, -ατος, τό, meal

κτάομαι (dep.), get, gain, acquire; (perf.) have acquired = possess, have

λέγω, λέξω/ἐρῶ, εἶπον, say

λέων, -οντος, ὁ, lion

μονόω, make solitary, leave alone

νομή, ἡ, pasturage, food from pasturing

ὄναγρος, ὁ, wild ass

ὀνηλάτης, -ου, ὁ, donkey-driver

ὄνος, ὁ/ἡ, ass

ὄντως (adv.), really, truly

ὁράω/ὁρῶ, ὄψομαι, εἶδον, see

ὄρος, -εος, τό, mountain, hill

ὅτι (causal particle), because, since

οὗτος, αὕτη, τοῦτο, this; (pl.) these

πληγή, ἡ, blow

προσπελάζω, draw near to, approach (+ dat.)

πτῶμα, -ατος, τό, corpse, carcass

σκληροτράχηλος, -ον, stiff-necked; inflexible; insubordinate

συμβαίνω, (3rd sing. often impersonal) come to pass, happen

σύνειμι, be with (+ dat.)

σφοδρῶς (adv.), violently

τίθημι, make X (acc.) Y (acc.)

τις, τι, (gen. τινος) (indef. adj.) a, an; any

τρέφω, (of slaves, cattle, dogs, etc.) rear and keep; feed

τυγχάνω, happen to be (+ dat.)

φαίνω, bring to light; (pass.) appear

φέρω, carry off or away

ὡς (particle w/ gen. abs.), see note above; (conj.; = ὅτι), that

Alexander Calder (1931)

19. The Wolf and the Wet Nurse
(Babrius 16 = Perry 158)

Ἄγροικος ἠπείλησε νηπίῳ τίτθῃ

κλαίοντι "σῖγα. μή σε τῷ λύκῳ ῥίψω."

λύκος δ' ἀκούσας τήν τε γραῦν ἀληθεύειν

νομίσας ἔμεινεν ὡς ἕτοιμα δειπνήσων,

5   ἕως ὁ παῖς μὲν ἑσπέρης ἐκοιμήθη,

αὐτὸς δὲ πεινῶν καὶ λύκος χανὼν ὄντως

ἀπῆλθε νωθραῖς ἐλπίσιν παρεδρεύσας.

λύκαινα δ' αὐτὸν ἡ σύνοικος ἠρώτα

"πῶς οὐδὲν ἦλθες ἄρας, ὡς πρὶν εἰώθεις;"

10   ὁ δ' εἶπε "πῶς γάρ, ὃς γυναικὶ πιστεύω;"

---

2   **σῖγα** 2nd sing. pres. act. impera. < σιγάω
     μή = ἵνα μή, 'lest' (+ subju. in primary sequence); negative purpose
     clause (Smyth § 2193)

3   **ἀκούσας** sc. these words/this

4   **δειπνήσων** fut. part. expresses purpose (Smyth § 2065)

5   **ἑσπέρης** gen. of time within which (Smyth § 1444)
     ἐκοιμήθη 3rd sing. aor. pass. indic. < κοιμάω

6   **λύκος χανὼν ὄντως** lit., 'truly a wolf w/ his mouth wide open,' a
     citation of the proverbial expression for disappointed hopes (λύκος ἔχανεν,
     'the wolf opened his mouth wide [sc. for nothing]') that was itself probably
     derived from an earlier version of this fable. Babrius's use of the proverbial
     expression within the fable that generated it is unique since no other variant
     employs the expression

7   **νωθραῖς ἐλπίσιν** dat. of accompanying circumstance/manner (Smyth §
     1527)

8   **λύκαινα...ἠρώτα** = δ' λύκαινα, ἡ σύνοικος, ἠρώτα αὐτὸν

9   **εἰώθεις** 2nd sing. pluperf. (w/ imperf. force) act. indic. < εἴωθα

10   **πῶς γάρ** 'for how (could I have brought something back)'

ἄγροικος, -ον, rustic, country-dwelling
αἴρω, ἀρῶ, ἦρα, take up and bring
ἀκούω, hear
ἀληθεύω, speak truth(fully)
ἀπειλέω, threaten (+ dat. of person)
ἀπέρχομαι, ἀπελεύσομαι,
  ἀπῆλθον, go away, depart
αὐτός, -ή, -ό, (adj.) -self, -selves;
  (pron. in gen., dat., acc.) him, her, it,
  them
γραῦς, γραός, ἡ, old woman
γυνή, -αικός, ἡ, woman
δειπνέω, make a meal of, dine on
εἴωθα (perf. used as pres.), be
  accustomed, be in the habit,
ἐλπίς, -ίδος, ἡ, hope, expectation
ἔρχομαι, ἐλεύσομαι, ἦλθον, come
ἐρωτάω, ask
ἑσπέρα, ἡ, evening
ἑτοῖμος, -ον, (of food) at hand,
  prepared; (of the fut.) sure to come,
  certain
ἕως (conj.), until
κλαίω, cry, wail
κοιμάω, put to sleep; (pass.) sleep
λύκαινα, ἡ, she-wolf
λύκος, ὁ, wolf
μένω, wait, stay where one is
νήπιος, τό, infant, child

νομίζω, believe that (+ acc. and inf.)
νωθρός, -ά, -όν, stupid
ὄντως (adv.), truly, really, actually
ὅς, ἥ, ὅ (rel. pron.), who, whose,
  whom, which, that
οὐδείς, οὐδεμία, οὐδέν, no one,
  nothing
παῖς, παιδός, ὁ/ἡ, child
παρεδρεύω, wait constantly
πεινάω, suffer hunger, be hungry or
  famished
πιστεύω, believe in, put one's trust
  or faith in (+ dat.)
πρίν (adv.), previously
πῶς, how? (sometimes to express
  displeasure) how is it that?
ῥίπτω, throw
σιγάω, be silent/quiet, keep silence
σύνοικος, -ον, dwelling in the
  same house w/ one
τε (particle/conj.), and
τίτθη, ἡ, wet nurse, i.e., a woman
  who (usually) breast feeds and cares
  for another's child
χάσκω, χανοῦμαι, ἔχανον, be
  agape, be w/ mouth wide open
ὡς (adv.), as, like; + fut. part., as if (to),
  in order to, to

Jacobs (1894)

"Be quiet now," said an old Nurse to a child sitting on her lap. "If you make that noise again I will throw you to the Wolf."

Now it chanced that a Wolf was passing close under the window as this was said. So he crouched down by the side of the house and waited. "I am in good luck to-day," thought he. "It is sure to cry soon, and a daintier morsel I haven't had for many a long day." So he waited, and he waited, and he waited, till at last the child began to cry, and the Wolf came forward before the window, and looked up to the Nurse, wagging his tail. But all the Nurse did was to shut down the window and call for help, and the dogs of the house came rushing out. "Ah," said the Wolf as he galloped away, "enemies promises were made to be broken."

J. Greenaway (1868)

Anonymous (1916)[10]

Giving the naughty child a shake, the Nurse said, "Now be good or else I'll throw you out the window to the Wolf." There really happened to be a Wolf lurking in the yard, and hearing the Nurse's words he got his appetite ready. There was nothing doing, however, so after a while the hungry Wolf gave it up and went home.

Some Foxes meeting the Wolf asked him why he looked so sad. "Because all men are liars—and some women, too," replied the disappointed Wolf.

MORAL: You can't believe what a nurse says: they are always talking about wolves and bogie men but they never produce them.

---

[10] From *Aesop's Fables with 100 Illustrations by F. Opper* (Philadelphia: J. B. Lippincott Company, 1916).

20. The Monkey and the Dolphin
(Chambry 306 = Perry 73)

Ἔθος ἐστὶ τοῖς πλέουσιν ἐπάγεσθαι κύνας Μελιταίους καὶ πιθήκους πρὸς παραμυθίαν τοῦ πλοῦ. Καὶ δή τις πλεῖν μέλλων πίθηκον συνανήνεγκε. Γενομένων δὲ αὐτῶν κατὰ Σούνιον - ἐστὶ δὲ τοῦτο Ἀθηνῶν ἀκρωτήριον - συνέβη χειμῶνα σφοδρὸν

5 γενέσθαι. Περιτραπείσης δὲ τῆς νηὸς καὶ πάντων διακολυμβώντων, καὶ ὁ πίθηκος ἐνήχετο. Δελφὶς δὲ θεασάμενος αὐτὸν καὶ οἰόμενος ἄνθρωπον εἶναι ὑπεξελθὼν διεκόμιζεν. Ὡς δὲ ἐγένετο κατὰ τὸν Πειραιᾶ, τὸν λιμένα τῶν Ἀθηνῶν, ἐπυνθάνετο τοῦ πιθήκου εἰ τὸ γένος Ἀθηναῖός ἐστι.

10 Τοῦ δὲ εἰπόντος καὶ λαμπρῶν ἐνταῦθα τετυχηκέναι γονέων, ἐκ δευτέρου ἤρετο αὐτὸν εἰ ἐπίσταται τὸν Πειραιᾶ. Καὶ ὃς ὑπολαβὼν αὐτὸν ἄνθρωπον λέγειν, ἔφασκε καὶ φίλον αὐτῷ καὶ συνήθη τοῦτον. Καὶ ὁ δελφὶς ἀγανακτήσας κατὰ τῆς αὐτοῦ ψευδολογίας βαπτίζων αὐτὸν ἀπέκτεινε.

15 Πρὸς ἄνδρα ψευδολόγον ὁ λόγος εὔκαιρος.

---

1 κύνας Μελιταίους small breed of dog well-known in the ancient world that was said by Strabo (64 BCE-24 CE) to be favored by noble women
2 πρὸς παραμυθίαν τοῦ πλοῦ i.e., to alleviate the boredom of a long journey
3 Σούνιον a promontory located c. 43 miles/69 kilometers south-southeast of Athens, at the southernmost tip of the Attica peninsula
4 Γενομένων...αὐτῶν gen. abs.
5-6 Περιτραπείσης...τῆς νηὸς, πάντων διακολυμβώντων gen. abs. x2
5 Περιτραπείσης fem. gen. sing. aor. pass. part. < περιτρέπω
9 τὸ γένος acc. of respect (Smyth § 1600)
10 Τοῦ δὲ εἰπόντος gen. abs., in which εἰπόντος governs two indir. statements: one implied (sc. 'that he was [Athenian]'), the other w/ perf. act. inf. τετυχηκέναι < τυγχάνω
11 Καὶ ὃς 'and he', occurs at the beginning of a clause in post-Homeric Gk. (in Homeric Greek ὅς, ἥ, ὅ were originally demonstrative pronouns)
12 αὐτῷ dat. of possession
15 ὁ λόγος εὔκαιρος sc. ἐστί

ἀγανακτέω, be angry; + κατά τινος, be angry at someone or something

Ἀθῆναι, -ῶν, αἱ, Athens

Ἀθηναῖος, -α, -ον, Athenian, of or from Athens

ἀκρωτήριον, τό, sea-promontory, cape

ἀνήρ, ἀνδρός, ὁ, man

ἄνθρωπος, ὁ, man, person

ἀποκτείνω, ἀποκτενῶ, ἀπέκτεινα, kill

αὐτός, -ή, -ό, (pron. in gen., dat., acc.) him, her, it, them

βαπτίζω, plunge X (acc.) under water

γένος, τό, race, stock, kin, ethnicity

γίγνομαι/γίνομαι, γενήσομαι, ἐγενόμην, be, come about

γονεύς, -έως, ὁ, father, begetter; (pl.) parents; ancestors

δελφίς, -ῖνος, ὁ, dolphin

δεύτερος, -α, -ον, second; ἐκ δευτέρου, 'next'

δή, (particle) indeed; in fact; καὶ δή, and on this particular occasion

διακολυμβάω, plunge; swim across

διακομίζω, carry over or across

ἔθος, -εος, τό, custom

εἰ (conj.), if

ἐνταῦθα (adv.), there

ἐπάγω, bring on; (mid.) bring w/ one

ἐπίσταμαι, know, be acquainted w/

ἔρομαι, εἰρήσομαι, ἠρόμην, ask

εὔκαιρος, -ον, suitable

θεάομαι, (dep.) look on, watch; see

κατά (prep. + acc.), by, at, along

κύων, κυνός, ὁ/ἡ, dog

λαμπρός, -ή, -όν, well-known, illustrious, famous

λέγω, λέξω/ἐρῶ, εἶπον, mean, speak of

λιμήν, -ένος, ὁ, harbor

λόγος, ὁ, story, tale

Μελιταῖος, -α, -ον, Maltese

μέλλω, be about to (usu. + fut. inf.; rarely w/ pres. inf.)

ναῦς, νεώς/νηός, ἡ, ship

νήχω/νήχομαι (act./mid. w/ same meaning), swim

οἴομαι, think

οὗτος, αὕτη, τοῦτο, this; (pl.) these

παραμυθία, ἡ, diversion, distraction

πᾶς, πᾶσα, πᾶν, all, every

Πειραιεύς, -έως, ὁ, Peiraeus

περιτρέπω, turn upside down, capsize

πίθηκος, ὁ, monkey, ape

πλέω, sail, go by sea

πλοῦς, πλοῦ, πλῷ, πλοῦν, ὁ, voyage

πρός (prep. + acc.), for

πυνθάνομαι, πεύσομαι, ἐπυθόμην, inquire of, ask (+ gen.)

Σούνιον, τό, Sounion, Sunium

συμβαίνω, συμβήσομαι, συνέβην (3rd sing. often impersonal) come to pass, happen (+ acc. and inf.)

συναναφέρω, συνανοίσω, συνανήνεγκα, bring w/ oneself

συνήθης, -ες, well-acquainted w/ (+ dat.); (as substantive) friend

σφοδρός, -ά, -όν, strong, violent

τις, τι (gen. τινος), (indefinite adj.) a certain; some; a, an, any

τυγχάνω, happen to have (+ gen.)

ὑπεξέρχομαι, -ειμι, -ῆλθον, go out to meet

ὑπολαμβάνω, -λήψομαι, -έλαβον, suppose, assume

φάσκω, say, assert (often w/ a notion of pretending)

φίλος, -η, -ον, dear, beloved; (as substantive) friend

χειμών, -ῶνος, ὁ, storm

ψευδολογία, ἡ, falsehood, false speech, telling lies

ψευδόλογος, -ον, speaking falsely, lying

ὡς (conj. + indic. past tense verb), when

L'Estrange (1692)

People were us'd in the Days of Old, to carry Gamesome *Puppies* and *Apes* with 'em out to Sea, to pass away the Time withal. Now there was One of these *Apes*, it seems, aboard a Vessel that was cast away in a very great Storm. As the Men were Padling for their Lives, and an *Ape* for Company, a certain *Dolphin* that took him for a Man, got him upon his Back, and was making towards Land with him. He had him into a safe Road call'd the *Pyraeus*, and took occasion to ask the *Ape* whether he was an *Athenian* or not? He told him Yes, and of a very Ancient Family there. Why then (says the *Dolphin*) you know *Pyraeus:* Oh! Exceedingly well, says t'other (taking it for the Name of a Man). Why *Pyraeus* is my particular good Friend. The *Dolphin* upon this, had such an Indignation for the Impudence of the *Buffoon-Ape*, that he gave him the Slip from between his Legs, and there was an end of my very good Friend, the *Athenian*.

THE MORAL. *Bragging, Lying, and Pretending, has Cost many a Man his Life and Estate.*

La Fontaine (1668)
(Hill [2008])

To occupy the boring weeks
On sailing voyages, the Greeks
Transported with them on the seas
Performing dogs and chimpanzees.
A ship with such a crew, they say,
Once sank on entering Athens bay,
And men and beasts within the briny
Would all have met unpleasant ends
But for the dolphins, man's wet friends –
'Tis true, they are – 'twas said by Pliny.
They rescued all with human shape;
Even the ugly, hairy ape
By anthropomorphicity
Received salvation from the sea.
A dolphin who had trouble seeing,
Mistaking an ape for a human being,
Bore him upon his back in style
Like Arion, once long before.
And then, as they drew near the shore,

The dolphin, with his charming smile,
Asked, "Sir, are you Athenian?"
"You bet," said the Ape, "a famous son.
If you're in town and need things done
Just use my name. My family line
Sits high in governmental ranks;
The mayor is a cousin of mine."
The dolphin said, "A thousand thanks!
And I suppose you know Piraeus?
You're well-acquainted, I would guess?"
The ape replied, "My goodness, yes!
When we get kidding, you should see us!"
Our gross buffoon by this retort
Confused a person with a port.
How often types like this don't know
Paris, France, from Kokomo.
They rattle on at rapid pace:
Of words, a lot: of thought, no trace.
The dolphin laughed, then turned his head
To better see his passenger.
He'd saved no human but, instead,
A poor dumb beast decked out in fur.
He shook him off and went to find
Someone worth saving – with a mind.

Arthur Rackham (1912)

G. Gouget (1833)

AN APE AND
A DOLPHIN

Stephen Gooden (1936)

21. The Man and the Oracle
(Chambry 50 [Variant 2] = Perry 36)

Ἀνὴρ κακοπράγμων εἰς τὸν ἐν Δελφοῖς ἧκεν Ἀπόλλωνα,
πειρᾶσαι τοῦτον βουλόμενος. Καὶ δὴ λαβὼν στρουθίον ἐν τῇ
χειρὶ καὶ τοῦτο τῇ ἐσθῆτι σκεπάσας, ἔστη τε τοῦ τρίποδος
ἔγγιστα καὶ ἤρετο τὸν θεὸν λέγων· "Ἄπολλον, ὅ μετὰ χεῖρας
5 φέρω, πότερον ἔμπνουν ἐστὶν ἢ ἄπνουν;" βουλόμενος, εἰ μὲν
ἄπνουν εἴποι, ζῶν ἀναδεῖξαι τὸ στρουθίον· εἰ δ᾽ ἔμπνουν,
εὐθὺς ἀποπνίξας νεκρὸν ἐκεῖνο προενεγκεῖν. Ὁ δέ γε θεὸς τὴν
κακότεχνον αὐτοῦ γνοὺς ἐπίνοιαν, εἶπεν. "Ὁπότερον, ὦ
οὗτος, βούλει ποιῆσαι, ποίησον· παρὰ σοὶ γὰρ κεῖται τοῦτο
10 πρᾶξαι ἤτοι ζῶν ὃ κατέχεις ἢ νεκρὸν ὑποδεῖξαι."

Ὁ μῦθος δηλοῖ ὅτι τὸ θεῖον ἀπαραλόγιστον καὶ ἀλάθητον.

---

3   τῇ ἐσθῆτι instrumental dat. (Smyth § 1503)
     ἔστη 3rd sing. aor. act. indic. < ἵστημι
     τοῦ τρίποδος a three-legged (lit., 'three-footed') cauldron; at Delphi,
     the cauldron from which the Delphic Priestess of Apollo delivered her
     oracles
4   κἀκεῖσε = καὶ + ἐκεῖσε
5-6 εἰ... εἴποι...ἀναδεῖξαι FLV condit., w/ inf. (as complement to
     βουλόμενος) in the apodosis
     εἴποι 3rd sing. aor. act. opt. < λέγω
8-9 ὦ οὗτος an emphatic form of address, generally implying anger
9   ποίησον 2nd sing. aor. act. impera. < ποιέω/ποιῶ
9-10 τοῦτο πρᾶξαι the inf. phrase is the subj. of κεῖται
10   ἤτοι...ὑποδεῖξαι this phrase is in apposition to τοῦτο πρᾶξαι

ἀλάθητος, -ον, not to be deceived

ἀναδείκνυμι, ἀναδείξω, ἀνέδειξα, lift up and show, exhibit, display

ἀνήρ, ἀνδρός, ὁ, man, husband

ἀπαραλόγιστος, -ον, not to be tricked

ἄπνους, -ουν, w/out breathing, lifeless, dead

Ἀπόλλων, -ωνος, ὁ, Apollo

ἀποπνίγω, choke, strangle

αὐτός, -ή, -ό, (pron. in gen., dat., acc.) him, her, it; them

βούλομαι, wish, want (+ inf.)

γε (enclitic particle, giving emphasis to the word or words which it follows, (except in the case of articles, in which case it emphasizes the word that follows it). With single words, 'at least,' 'at any rate,' but often only to be rendered by italics in writing, or emphasis in pronunciation)

γι(γ)νώσκω, γνώσομαι, ἔγνων, know, perceive, discern

Δελφοί, -ῶν, οἱ, Delphi

δή (particle), indeed, in fact

δηλόω, show, reveal

ἔγγιστα (adv./prep. + gen.), very close to, very near to

εἰ (conj.), if

ἐκεῖνος, ἐκείνη, ἐκεῖνο, that; (pl.) those

ἔμπνους, -ουν, breathing, living, alive

ἐπίνοια, ἡ, purpose, plan

ἔρομαι, εἰρήσομαι, ἠρόμην, ask, inquire of

ἐσθής, -ῆτος, ἡ, clothes

εὐθύς (adv.), immediately, at once

ζάω/ζῶ, live

ἥκω (pres.), have come; ἧκον (imperf.), had come, came

ἤτοι...ἤ (conjs.), either...or

θεῖον, τό, divinity, the divine

θεός, ὁ, god

ἵστημι, make X stand; stop X; set X (up); (2nd aor.; perf.) stand

κακοπράγμων, -ον, doing evil, wicked

κακότεχνος, -ον, artful; fraudulent

κατέχω, hold tightly; possess, have in one's possession

κεῖμαι, lie; + παρά τινι, be in the power of X, rest entirely w/ X, be dependent on X

λαμβάνω, λήψομαι, ἔλαβον, take, seize

λέγω, λέξω/ἐρῶ, εἶπον, say

μετά (prep. + acc.), between, in

μῦθος, ὁ, story, fable, tale

νεκρός, -ή, -όν, dead

ὁπότερος, -η, -ον, whichever (of two things/possibilities)

ὅς, ἥ, ὅ (rel. pron.), who, whose, whom, which, that

ὅτι (conj.), that

οὗτος, αὕτη, τοῦτο, this; (pl.) these

πειράω, test, put X (acc.) to the test

ποιέω/ποιῶ, do

πότερον...ἤ (adv./conj.), (whether)... or

πράττω, do, accomplish

πρός (prep. + acc.), for

προφέρω, προοίσω, προήνεγκον, bring forth, present; display

σκεπάζω, cover; hide, conceal

στρουθίον, τό, sparrow

τε καί/τε...καί, (both)...and

τρίπους, -ποδος, ὁ, tripod

ὑποδείκνυμι, ὑποδείξω, ὑπέδειξα, show, bring to light

φέρω, carry

χείρ, χειρός, ἡ, hand

ὡς (conj.), that

22. The Eagle and His Captor
(Chambry 6 [Variant 2]/6 = Perry 275)

Ποτὲ ἀετὸς ἑάλω ὑπ' ἀνθρώπου. Τούτου δὲ τὰ πτερὰ ὁ ἄνθρωπος κόψας ἀφῆκε μετὰ τῶν ὀρνίθων ἐν οἴκῳ εἶναι. Ὁ δὲ ἦν κατηφὴς καὶ οὐδὲν ἤσθιεν ἐκ τῆς λύπης. ὅμοιος δὲ ἦν βασιλεῖ δεσμώτῃ. Ἕτερος δέ τις τοῦτον ὠνησάμενος καὶ τὰ
5 πτερὰ ἀνασπάσας καὶ μύρῳ χρίσας ἐποίησε πτερῶσαι. Ὁ δὲ πετασθεὶς καὶ τοῖς ὄνυξι λαγωὸν ἁρπάσας ἤνεγκεν αὐτῷ δῶρον. Ἀλώπηξ δὲ ἰδοῦσα εἶπεν "Μὴ τούτῳ δίδου, ἀλλὰ τῷ πρώτῳ, ὅτι ὁ μὲν φύσει ἀγαθός ἐστιν. Ἐκεῖνον δὲ μᾶλλον ἐξευμενίζου, μή πως πάλιν λαβών σε τῶν πτερῶν
10 ἐρημώσῃ."

Ὅτι δεῖ χρηστὰς ἀμοιβὰς τοῖς εὐεργέταις παρέχειν, τοὺς πονηροὺς δὲ φρονίμως τροποῦσθαι.

---

5 ἐποίησε πτερῶσαι periphrasis for ἐπτέρωσε
   μύρῳ instrumental dat. (Smyth § 1503)
6 πετασθεὶς masc. nom. sing. aor. pass. part. < πετάννυμι/πετάω
   τοῖς ὄνυξι instrumental dat. (Smyth § 1503)
   ἤνεγκεν 3rd sing. aor. act. indic. < φέρω
7 ἰδοῦσα fem. nom. sing. aor. act. part. < ὁράω/ὁρῶ
   δίδου 2nd sing. pres. act. imper. < δίδωμι
8 ὁ μὲν i.e., the second man, who restored the eagle's wings
9 ἐξευμενίζου 2nd sing. pres. act. imper. < ἐξευμενίζω
9-10 μή...ἐρημώσῃ neg. purpose clause (Smyth § 1503), i.e., lest...
   ἐρημώσῃ 3rd sing. aor. act. subju. < ἐρημόω
11 Ὅτι = Ὁ μῦθος/λόγος δηλοῖ ὅτι

Contradictory Morals

Gibbs (44) notes that: "The moral added to this fable flatly contradicts the moral inside the fable pronounced by the fox. The fox is pragmatic: give the reward to the wicked man in order to win his favour. The editor of the fable prefers a more pious rule of behavior: good deeds, not wickedness, should be rewarded."

ἀγαθός, -ή, -όν, good
ἀετός, ὁ, eagle
ἁλίσκομαι, ἁλώσομαι, ἑάλων, be
  caught
ἀλώπηξ, -εκος, ἡ, fox
ἀμοιβή, ἡ, repayment, compensation,
  recompense
ἀνασπάω, pull up
ἄνθρωπος, ὁ, man, person
ἁρπάζω, snatch up, carry off
αὐτός, -ή, -ό, (pron. in gen., dat.,
  acc.) him, her, it; them
ἀφίημι, ἀφήσω, ἀφῆκα, send forth;
  leave alone; allow
βασιλεύς, -έως, ὁ, king
δεῖ, one must or ought (+ inf.)
δεσμώτης, -ου, ὁ, prisoner; (as adj.)
  in chains
δηλόω, show, reveal
δίδωμι, δώσω, ἔδωκα, give
δῶρον, τό, gift
ἐκ (prep. + gen.), because of, on
  account of
ἐκεῖνος, ἐκείνη, ἐκεῖνο, that; (pl.)
  those
ἐξευμενίζω, (mid. w/ same meaning
  as act.) propitiate
ἐρημόω, deprive X (acc.) of Y (gen.)
ἐσθίω, eat
ἕτερος, -α, -ον, other, another
εὐεργέτης, -ου, ὁ, benefactor
κατηφής, -ές, downcast, feeling
  despondent
κόπτω, cut off
λαγῶς, ὁ, hare
λαμβάνω, λήψομαι, ἔλαβον, seize,
  take
λέγω, λέξω/ἐρῶ, εἶπον, say
λόγος, ὁ, tale, story
λύπη, ἡ, grief, sad plight or condition

μᾶλλον (adv.), + δέ, but rather
μετά (prep. + gen.), with
μῦθος, ὁ, story, fable, tale
μύρον, τό, sweet oil, ointment
οἶκος, ὁ, house; cage for birds
ὅμοιος, -α, -ον, like (+ dat.)
ὄνυξ, -υχος, ὁ, talon
ὁράω/ὁρῶ, ὄψομαι, εἶδον, see
ὄρνις, ὄρνιθος, ὁ/ἡ, bird
ὅτι (conj.), because; that
οὐδείς, οὐδεμία, οὐδέν, no one,
  nothing
οὗτος, αὕτη, τοῦτο, this; (pl.) those
πάλιν (adv.), again, once more
παρέχω, present, offer, give
πετάννυμι/πετάω, spread open/wide;
  (pass.) fly, take flight
ποιέω, accomplish, bring about
πονηρός, -ά, -όν, wicked, bad
ποτε (adv.), at some time, at
  one time, once (upon a time)
πρῶτος, -η, -ον, first
πτερόν, τό, feather
πτερόω, furnish w/ feathers or wings
πως (particle), somehow, in some way
τις, τι, (gen. τινος) (indef. adj.) a
  certain; some; a, an; (indef. pron.)
  someone; something; anyone;
  anything
τροπέω, turn; (mid.) turn (away from)
  and flee
ὑπό (prep. + gen.), (w/ pass. voice) by
φέρω, οἴσω, ἤνεγκον, carry, bring
φρονίμως (adv.), sensibly, prudently
φύσις, φύσεως, ἡ, nature; (dat.) by
  nature
χρηστός, -ή, -όν, good, useful
χρίω, rub or anoint w/ oil or ointment
ὠνέομαι, buy, purchase

23. The Tortoise and the Hare
(Chambry 353 [Variant 2] = Perry 226)

Ποδῶν χελώνης κατεγέλα λαγωός. Ἡ δὲ ἔφη· "Ἐγώ σε
τὸν ταχύποδα νικήσω." Ὁ δέ· "Λόγῳ μόνῳ λέγεις τοῦτο·
ἀλλ᾽ ἔριζε καὶ γνῶθι." – "Τίς δὲ τὸν τόπον ὁρίσει," ἔφη,
"καὶ βραβεύσει τὴν νίκην;" – "Ἀλώπηξ," ἔφη, "ἡ δικαία καὶ
5 σοφωτάτη." Ἔταξε δὲ τὴν ἀρχὴν τῆς ὥρας τοῦ δρόμου. Ἡ δὲ
χελώνη μὴ ῥᾳθυμήσασα ἤρξατο τῆς ὁδοῦ. Ὁ δὲ λαγωὸς τοῖς
ποσὶ θαρρῶν ἐκοιμήθη. Ἐλθὼν δὲ ἐπὶ τὸν ὡρισμένον τόπον
εὗρε τὴν χελώνην νικήσασαν.

Ὅτι πολλαὶ φύσεις ἀνθρώπων εὐφυεῖς εἰσιν, ἀλλ᾽ ἐκ τῆς
10 ῥᾳθυμίας ἀπώλοντο, ἐκ δὲ νήψεως καὶ σπουδῆς καὶ
μακροθυμίας τινὲς καὶ φύσεως ἀργῆς περιεγένοντο.

---

2 **τὸν ταχύποδα** in apposition to σε
Λόγῳ μόνῳ instrumental dat. (Smyth § 1507)
Λόγῳ...λέγεις a rhetorical trope known as *figura etymologica*, in which a vb. governs its related noun

3 **ἔριζε** 2nd sing. pres. impera. < ἐρίζω; sc. w/ me
γνῶθι 2nd sing. aor. impera. < γι(γ)νώσκω; sc. who is faster

4-5 **Ἀλώπηξ...ἡ δικαία καὶ σοφωτάτη** sc. ἐστί; a joke, since in the Aesopic fable tradition, while foxes are famously clever, they are never portrayed as 'δικαία'

6 **μὴ** + part. here w/ causal force (cf. Smyth § 2731)

7 **ἐκοιμήθη** 3rd sing. aor. pass. indic. < κοιμάω
τὸν ὡρισμένον τόπον i.e., the finish line
ὡρισμένον masc. acc. sing. perf. mid./pass. part. < ὁρίζω

9 **Ὅτι** = Ὁ μῦθος/λόγος δηλοῖ ὅτι

10-11 **ἀπώλοντο... περιεγένοντο** gnomic aorists (Smyth § 1931); translate as pres. tense

11 **καὶ** (here w/ adverbial force) 'even'
φύσεως ἀργῆς sc. their own

ἀλλά (conj.), but (stronger than δέ)

ἀλώπηξ, ἀλώπεκος, ἡ, fox

ἄνθρωπος, ὁ, man, person

ἀπολλύμι, ἀπολέσω/ἀπολῶ, ἀπώλεσα, destroy, kill; (mid.) be ruined

ἀργός, -ή, -όν, idle, lazy

ἀρχή, ἡ, beginning

ἄρχω, (act./mid.) begin, make a beginning of (+ gen.); + ὁδοῦ, lead the way

βραβεύω, decide on

γι(γ)νώσκω, learn, come to know

δηλόω, show, reveal

δίκαιος, -α, -ον, just, fair

δρόμος, ὁ, race

ἐκ (prep. + gen.), from, by

ἐπί (prep. + acc.), to

ἐρίζω, contend, compete, challenge

ἔρχομαι, ἐλεύσομαι, ἦλθον, come

εὑρίσκω, εὑρήσω, ηὗρον/εὗρον, find

εὐφυής, -ές, well-developed, well-formed; of good natural disposition or ability, gifted with a good quality

θαρρέω, have confidence in (+ dat.)

καταγελάω, laugh at, mock (+ gen.)

κοιμάω, put to sleep; (mid./pass.) fall asleep, lay down to sleep/take a nap

λαγωός/λαγῶς, ὁ, hare

λέγω, say

λόγος, ὁ, words, verbal expression

μακροθυμία, ἡ, patient self-control, patience; restraint and tolerance under provocation

μονός, -ή, -όν, alone, only

νῆψις, -εως, ἡ, sobriety (i.e., the state of being earnestly thoughtful, calm, modest, and possessing sound judgement)

νικάω, defeat, conquer, vanquish (+ acc.); prevail, win

νίκη, ἡ, victory

ὁδός, ὁδοῦ, ἡ, road, way, journey

ὁρίζω, ὁριῶ/ὁρίσω, ὥρισα, mark out by boundaries; determine

ὅτι (conj.), that

οὗτος, αὕτη, τοῦτο, this; (pl.) these

περιγί(γ)νομαι, περιγενήσομαι, περιεγενόμην, overcome (+ gen.)

πολύς, πολλή, πολύ, much; (pl.) many

πούς, πόδος, ὁ, foot

ῥᾳθυμέω/ῥαθυμέω, be idle

ῥᾳθυμία, ἡ, laziness, idleness

σοφός, -ή, -όν, wise; clever

σπουδή, ἡ, zeal, great exertion

τάσσω, τάξω, ἔταξα, appoint, prescribe, set

ταχύπους, ταχύπουν, (gen. ταχύποδος), swift-footed

τις, τι (gen. τινος), (indefinite adj.) a certain; some; a, an, any

τίς, τί (gen. τίνος; interrog. pron. and adj.), who? which? what?

τόπος, ὁ, place

φημί, φήσω, ἔφην, say

φύσις, -εως, ἡ, (one's) nature, natural quality, disposition, or ability

χελώνη, ἡ, tortoise

ὥρα, ἡ, time for (+ gen.)

THE HARE & THE TORTOISE

Richard Heighway (1894)

L'Estrange (1692)

What a dull heavy Creature (says a *Hare*) is this same *Tortoise!* And yet (says the *Tortoise*) I'll run with you for a Wager. 'Twas *done and done*, and the *Fox*, by Consent, was to be the Judge. They started together, and the *Tortoise* kept jogging on still till he came to the End of the Course. The *Hare* laid himself down about Midway, and took a Nap; for, says he, I can fetch up the *Tortoise* when I please: But he over-slept himself, it seems, for when he came to wake, though he scudded away as fast as 'twas possible, the *Tortoise* got to the Post before him, and won the Wager.

THE MORAL. *Up and be doing, is an edifying Text; for Action is the Business of Life, and there's no Thought of ever coming to the End of our Journey in time, if we sleep by the Way.*

Anonymous (1857)[11]

"WHAT a dull, heavy creature," said a bright-eyed, nimble-footed Hare, "is this same plodding Tortoise! He trudges along in the mud, neither looking to the right nor to the left, only caring to nibble such of the dryest grass and the dirtiest roots as come in his way, and making no more progress in a day's march than I can accomplish in two or three careless bounds!"

"And yet," said the Tortoise (in whose hearing the speech had been made for his humiliation), "although I have neither your lightness of foot, nor the compact and powerful symmetry of your haunches, I will undertake to run you for a wager."

"Agreed," said the Hare, contemptuously. So a goal was named, and away they started together. The Tortoise kept jogging along at his usual rate, and was soon left behind and out of sight by the Hare, who, tired of running alone in a given direction, fell to browsing on choice plants, and then went off to a game of play with certain of his sportive companions, finally making up his form for a snug nap among some tempting long autumn grass: "For," said he, "with my great natural gift of swiftness, I

---

[11] From *The Fables of Aesop and Others Translated into Human Nature. Designed and Drawn on the Wood by Charles H. Bennett.* London: W. Kent & Co., 1857.

can fetch up Old Humdrum Master Tortoise whenever I please."

But he overslept himself, it seems. For when he came to wake, it was already dark, the weather had changed, and the fields were heavy with clay; and though he scudded away as fast as the ground would let him, he was fain to drop at last half dead with cold and fatigue in sight of the winning-post, which the Tortoise had reached comfortably before him,-- thereby winning the wager.

MORAL.

Genius that may outrun the Constable, cannot overtake Time lost.

Charles H. Bennett (1857)

85

Townsend (1867)

A HARE one day ridiculed the short feet and slow pace of the Tortoise, who replied, laughing: 'Though you be swift as the wind, I will beat you in a race.' The Hare, believing her assertion to be simply impossible, assented to the proposal; and they agreed that the Fox should choose the course and fix the goal. On the day appointed for the race the two started together. The Tortoise never for a moment stopped, but went on with a slow but steady pace straight to the end of the course. The Hare, lying down by the wayside, fell fast asleep. At last waking up, and moving as fast as he could, he saw the Tortoise had reached the goal, and was comfortably dozing after her fatigue.

Slow but steady wins the race.

Linton (1887)

Twas a race between Tortoise and Hare,
Puss was sure she'd so much time to spare,
That she lay down to sleep,
And let old Thick-shell creep
To the winning-post first! – You may stare.

PERSISTENCE BEATS IMPULSE

Jacobs (1894)

The Hare was once boasting of his speed before the other animals. "I have never yet been beaten," said he, "when I put forth my full speed. I challenge any one here to race with me."

The Tortoise said quietly, "I accept your challenge."

"That is a good joke," said the Hare; "I could dance round you all the way."

"Keep your boasting till you've beaten," answered the Tortoise. "Shall we race?"

So a course was fixed and a start was made. The Hare darted almost out of sight at once, but soon stopped and, to show his contempt for the Tortoise, lay down to have a nap. The Tortoise plodded on and plodded on, and when the Hare awoke from his nap, he saw the Tortoise just near the winning-post and could not run up in time to save the race. Then said the Tortoise:

"Plodding wins the race."

Richard Heighway (1894)

24. The Lion and the Farmer's Daughter
(Chambry 199/198 = Perry 140)

Λέων ἐρασθεὶς γεωργοῦ θυγατρὸς, ταύτην ἐμνηστεύσατο.
Ὁ δὲ μὴ ἐκδοῦναι θηρίῳ τὴν θυγατέρα ὑπομένων, μηδὲ
ἀρνήσασθαι διὰ φόβον δυνάμενος τοιοῦτόν τι ἐπενόησεν.
Ἐπειδὴ συνεχῶς αὐτῷ ὁ λέων ἐπέκειτο, ἔλεγεν ὡς νυμφίον
5   μὲν αὐτὸν ἄξιον τῆς θυγατρὸς δοκιμάζει· μὴ ἄλλως δὲ αὐτῷ
δύνασθαι ἐκδοῦναι, ἐὰν μὴ τούς τε ὀδόντας ἐξέλῃ καὶ τοὺς
ὄνυχας ἐκτέμῃ· τούτους γὰρ δεδοικέναι τὴν κόρην. Τοῦ δὲ
ῥᾳδίως διὰ τὸν ἔρωτα ἑκάτερα ὑπομείναντος, ὁ γεωργὸς
καταφρονήσας αὐτοῦ, ὡς παρεγένετο πρὸς αὐτόν, ῥοπάλοις
10 αὐτὸν παίων ἐξήλασεν.

Ὁ λόγος δηλοῖ ὅτι οἱ ῥᾳδίως τοῖς πέλας πιστεύοντες,
ὅταν τῶν ἰδίων πλεονεκτημάτων ἑαυτοὺς ἀπογυμνώσωσιν,
εὐάλωτοι τούτοις γίνονται οἷς πρότερον φοβεροὶ
καθεστήκεσαν.

2-3 μὴ... μηδὲ + part. here w/ causal force (cf. Smyth § 2731)
ἐκδοῦναι aor. act. inf. < ἐκδίδωμι

4-7 ἔλεγεν note two different indir. statement constructions set up by this vb.:
(1) w/ conj. + indic. vb. (ὡς...δοκιμάζει); (2) w/ two infinitives (δύνασθαι in
line 6, δεδοικέναι in line 7)

6 ἐὰν μὴ...ἐξέλῃ...ἐκτέμῃ protasis of a FLV condit.; apodosis is in the
indir. statement μὴ...δύνασθαι ἐκδοῦναι
ἐὰν = εἰ + ἄν, 'unless' (+ subju.)

7 δεδοικέναι perf. (w/ force of pres.) act. inf. < δείδω

7-8 Τοῦ...ὑπομείναντος gen. abs.

9 ῥοπάλοις instrumental dat. (Smyth § 1503)

12 ὅταν...ἀπογυμνώσωσιν... γίνονται pres. general condit.
ὅταν = ὅτε + ἄν, 'whenever' (+ subju.)

13 τούτοις dat. of the agent w/ verbal adj. (here εὐάλωτοι) (Smyth § 1488a)

14 καθεστήκεσαν 3rd pl. pluperf. (w/ force of imperf.) act. indic. <
καθίστημι

ἄλλως (adv.), otherwise

ἄξιος, -ία, -ιον, worthy of (+ gen.)

ἀπογυμνόω, strip X (acc.) bare of Y (gen.)

ἀρνέομαι, refuse, say 'no'

αὐτός, -ή, -ό, (pron. in gen., dat., acc.) him, her, it; them

γεωργός, ὁ, farmer

γί(γ)νομαι, become

δείδω, fear

δηλόω, show, reveal

διά (prep. + acc.), because of

δοκιμάζω, approve (after scrutiny as fit), think fit

δύναμαι, be able (+ inf.)

ἑαυτοῦ, -ῆς, -οῦ (reflex. pron. in gen., dat., acc.), himself, herself, itself; themselves

ἑκάτερος -,α, -ον, each of two, both

ἐκδίδωμι, ἐκδώσω, ἐξέδωκα, give up, surrender; + θυγατέρα, give one's daughter in marriage

ἐκτέμνω, ἐκτεμῶ, ἐξέτεμον, cut out

ἐξαιρέω, ἐξαιρήσω, ἐξεῖλον, take out, remove

ἐξελαύνω, ἐξελάσω/ἐξελῶ, ἐξήλασα, drive out

ἐπειδή (conj.), since

ἐπίκειμαι, press upon, urgently entreat one (+ dat.)

ἐπινοέω, contrive, devise

ἔραμαι, ἐρασθήσομαι, ἠράσθην, love, fall in love w/, desire passionately, lust after (+ gen.)

ἐράω, love, be in love w/ (+ gen.)

ἔρως, -ωτος, ὁ, love, passionate desire

εὐάλωτος, -ον, easy to be taken or caught

θηρίον, τό, wild animal, (savage) beast

θυγάτηρ, θυγατέρος/θυγατρός, ἡ, daughter

ἴδιος, -α, -ον, one's own

καθίστημι, bring into a certain state; (perf.) come into a certain state, become; (2nd aor. and pluperf.) be

καταφρονέω, look down on, think slightly of (+ gen.)

κόρη, ἡ, girl

λέγω, say

λέων, -οντος, ὁ, lion

λόγος, ὁ, tale, story

μνηστεύω, woo, court, seek in marriage

μῦθος, ὁ, story, fable, tale

νυμφίος, ὁ, bridegroom

ὀδούς, -όντος, ὁ, tooth

ὄνυξ, -υχος, ὁ, claw

ὅς, ἥ, ὅ (rel. pron.), who, whose, whom, which, that

ὅτι (conj.), that

οὗτος, αὕτη, τοῦτο, this; (pl.) these

παίω, strike, hit hard

παραγί(γ)νομαι, -γενήσομαι, παρεγενόμην, come to

πέλας (adv.), near, close; οἱ πέλας (sc. ὄντες), one's neighbors, one's fellow creatures, all men

πιστεύω, believe in, put one's trust or faith in (+ dat.)

πλεονέκτημα, -ατος, τό, advantage, superior quality

πρότερον (adv.), previously, before, earlier

ῥᾳδίως (adv.), easily

ῥόπαλον, τό, club, cudgel (used to beat donkeys/asses/mules)

συνεχῶς (adv.), continually, continuously, constantly

τε καί/τε...καί, (both)...and

τις, τι, (gen. τινος) (indef. pron.) someone; something; anyone; anything

τοιοῦτος, -αύτη, -οῦτον, such as this

ὑπομένω, ὑπομενῶ, ὑπέμεινα, submit to, endure; dare to do a thing (+ inf.)

φοβερός, -ή, -όν, causing fear, dreadful, terrible, formidable

φόβος, ὁ, fear

ὡς (conj.; = ὅτι), that; (+ indic. past tense vb.) when

25. The Lion Falls in Love
(Aphthonius 7 = Perry 140)

Μῦθος ὁ τῆς παρθένου καὶ τοῦ λέοντος ἡδονῶν ἀποτρέπων.

Λέων ἤρα παρθένου καὶ προσελθὼν τῷ πατρὶ τῆς παιδὸς ἐγγυῆσαι τὴν κόρην πρὸς γάμον ἐδεῖτο. δεδιὼς δὲ ὁ
5 πατὴρ ἀπανήνασθαι, μετὰ τῶν ὀδόντων ἐκβαλεῖν ἐπειρᾶτο τοὺς ὄνυχας, μὴ ταῦτα — λέγων — φόβον τῇ παιδὶ κατεργάσηται· καὶ πεισθεὶς ὁ λέων ὑπ' ἔρωτος, ἀμυντηρίων πρόσεισι γυμνός, προσιὼν δὲ ῥοπάλοις τὴν τελευτὴν ἀντηλλάσσετο.
10 Ἐχθροῖς πειθαρχῶν ὑποστήσῃ τὸν κίνδυνον.

1-2   This sentence functions both as title and promythion; sc. 'is about' after λέοντος

1   ὁ τῆς παρθένου καὶ τοῦ λέοντος in apposition to Μῦθος

2   ἀποτρέπων sc. us or one

4   δεδιὼς masc. nom. sing. perf. (w/force of pres.) act. part. < δείδω

5   μετὰ...πειρᾶτο a very elliptical phrase; sc. 'to persuade him,' 'to get him to agree' after ἐπειρᾶτο

6   μὴ = ἵνα μή, 'lest' (+ subju. in secondary sequence); negative purpose clause (Smyth § 2193)
   ταῦτα neut. pl. subj. w/ sing. vb. is very common in Gk. (Smyth § 958)

7-8   πρόσεισι...προσιὼν note repetition of same vb. (πρόσειμι) w same subj. (the lion), first as indic. then as part.

8   ῥοπάλοις instrumental dat. (Smyth § 1503)

9   ἀντηλλάσσετο sc. his prospects for marriage

10   πειθαρχῶν ὑποστήσῃ FMV condit., w/ part. as protasis, i.e., if you...
   ὑποστήσῃ 2nd sing. fut. mid./pass. indic. < ὑφίστημι

ἀμυντήριον, τό, means of protection, defense

ἀνταλλάσσω, (more freq. in mid.) exchange (one thing) w/ (another); receive X (acc.) in exchange

ἀπαναίνομαι, reject, deny, spurn, refuse

ἀποτρέπω, turn away from, dissuade from (+ gen.)

γάμος, ὁ, marriage

γυμνός, -ή, -όν, stripped of (+ gen.)

δείδω, fear to do (+ inf.)

δέομαι, ask or beg X (gen.) to do Y (inf.)

ἐγγυάω, (of a father) give his (daughter) in marriage, betroth

ἐκβάλλω, ἐκβαλῶ, ἐξέβαλον, cast or throw out/away, lose

ἐράω, love, be in love w/ (+ gen.)

ἔρως, -ωτος, ὁ, love, passionate desire

ἐχθρός, ὁ, one's enemy

ἡδονή, ἡ, pleasure, desire; (pl.) pleasures, desires, pleasant lusts

κατεργάζομαι, κατεργάσομαι, κατειργασάμην, produce, cause

κίνδυνος, ὁ, danger

κόρη, ἡ, girl

λέγω, say

λέων, -οντος, ὁ, lion

μετά (prep. + gen.), with, along with

μῦθος, ὁ, story, fable, tale

ὀδούς, -όντος, ὁ, tooth

ὄνυξ, -υχος, ὁ, claw

οὗτος, αὗτη, τοῦτο, this; (pl.) these

παῖς, παιδός, ὁ/ἡ, child

παρθένος, -ου, ἡ, maiden, girl

πατήρ, πατρός, ὁ, father

πειθαρχέω, obey, are obedient to, follow (the commands of) (+ dat.)

πείθω, persuade; (mid./pass.) listen to, obey (+ dat.)

πειράομαι, attempt, endeavor, try (+ inf.)

πρός (prep. + acc.), for the purpose of, for

πρόσειμι, come to, approach

προσέρχομαι, πρόσειμι, προσῆλθον, come to, approach

ῥόπαλον, τό, club, cudgel (used to beat donkeys/asses/mules)

τελευτή, ἡ, end of life, death

ὑπό, (prep. + gen. w/ pass. voice) by, under the influence of

ὑφίστημι, ὑποστήσω, ὑπέστησα, place under; (pass. + τὸν κίνδυνον) put oneself in, undertake unwillingly

φόβος, ὁ, fear

Richard Heighway (1894)

91

26. The Lion and the Old Man's Daughter
(Babrius 98 = Perry 140)

Λέων ἁλοὺς ἔρωτι παιδὸς ὡραίης

παρὰ πατρὸς ἐμνήστευε. τῷ δ' ὁ πρεσβύτης

οὐδέν τι δύσνουν οὐδ' ὕπουλον ἐμφήνας

"δίδωμι γῆμαι" φησι "καὶ διδοὺς χαίρω·

5   τίς οὐ δυνάστῃ καὶ λέοντι κηδεύσει;

φρένες δὲ δειλαὶ παρθένων τε καὶ παίδων·

σὺ δ' ἡλίκους μὲν ὄνυχας, ἡλίκους δ' ἥμιν

φέρεις ὀδόντας, τίς κόρη σε τολμήσει

ἀφόβως περιλαβεῖν; τίς δ' ἰδοῦσα μὴ κλαύσῃ;

10   πρὸς ταῦτα δὴ σκόπησον, εἰ γάμου χρῄζεις,

μηδ' ἄγριος θὴρ ἀλλὰ νυμφίος γίνου."

ὁ δὲ πτερωθεὶς τῇ δόσει τε πιστεύσας

ἐξεῖλε τοὺς ὀδόντας, εἶθ' ὑπὸ σμίλης

ἀπωνυχίσθη, τῷ τε πενθερῷ δείξας

15   τὴν παῖδ' ἀπῄτει. τὸν δ' ἕκαστος ἠλοία,

ῥοπάλῳ τις ἢ λίθῳ τις ἐκ χερὸς παίων,

[Continued on page 94]

---

1   ἁλοὺς masc. nom. sing. aor. act. part. < ἁλίσκομαι

2   τῷ = αὐτῷ. And in l. 15, τὸν = αὐτὸν

4   γῆμαι aor. act. inf. < γαμέω

6   φρένες δὲ δειλαὶ sc. εἰσί

7   ἥμιν dat. as indir. obj. but also, perhaps, of disadvantage, i.e., 'against us' (Smyth § 1481)

9   τίς δ' ἰδοῦσα = τίς δ' (κόρη) ἰδοῦσα (σε)
     κλαύσῃ 3rd sing. aor. act. subju. < κλαίω

10 σκόπησον 2nd sing. aor. act. impera. < σκοπέω

10-11 εἰ...χρῄζεις, μηδ'...γίνου pres. particular condit.

11 γίνου 2nd sing. pres. dep. impera. < γί(γ)νομαι

12 πτερωθεὶς masc. nom. sing. aor. pass. part. < πτερόω

14 ἀπωνυχίσθη 3rd sing. aor. pass. indic. < ἀπονυχίζω
     δείξας here the act. must have a mid.-reflex. sense

15 ἕκαστος sc. of the father's servants

ἄγριος, -ον, wild

ἁλίσκομαι, ἁλώσομαι, ἥλων/ἑάλων, be caught or seized by (+ dat.)

ἀλοάω/ἀλοιάω, beat, thrash, cudgel

ἀπαιτέω, ask for; demand back, demand to have returned (esp. of things rightfully belonging to one)

ἀπονυχίζω, trim or cut one's nails

αὐτός, -ή, -ό, (pron. in gen., dat., acc.) him, her, it; them

ἀφόβως (adv.), w/out fear

γαμέω, marry

γάμος, ὁ, marriage

γί(γ)νομαι, be

δείκνυμι, δείξω, ἔδειξα, show, exhibit

δειλός, -ή, -όν, cowardly

δή (particle), now, in truth, indeed

δίδωμι, give; (of parents) give one's daughter in marriage

δόσις, -εως, ἡ, permission; gift

δυνάστης, -ου, -ὁ, lord, master, ruler

δύσνους, -ουν, malevolent, hostile, bearing ill-will

εἶτα (adv.), then, next, after that

ἕκαστος, -η, -ον, each one, every one

ἐμφαίνω, -φανῶ, ἐνέφηνα, exhibit, display

ἐξαιρέω, ἐξαιρήσω, ἐξεῖλον, take out, remove

ἔρως, -ωτος, ὁ, love, passionate desire of/for (+ gen.)

ἤ (conj.), or

ἡλίκος, -η, -ον , how large, how great

θήρ, θηρός, ὁ, beast of prey (esp. of a lion), wild beast

κηδεύω, contract a marriage w/, ally oneself in marriage w/ (+ dat.)

κλαίω, κλαύσομαι, ἔκλαυσα, cry, wail

κόρη, ἡ, girl

λέων, -οντος, ὁ, lion

λίθος, ὁ, stone

μνηστεύω, seek in marriage

νυμφίος, ὁ, bridegroom

ὀδούς, -όντος, ὁ, tooth

ὄνυξ, -υχος, ὁ, claw

ὁρῶ, ὄψομαι, εἶδον, see

οὐδείς, οὐδεμία, οὐδέν, no one, nothing, no

οὗτος, αὕτη, τοῦτο, this; (pl.) these

παῖς, παιδός, ὁ/ἡ, child

παίω, strike, hit hard

παρά (prep. + gen.), from

παρθένος, ἡ, maiden, girl

πατήρ, πατρός, ὁ, father

πενθερός, ὁ, father-in-law

περιλαμβάνω, περιλήψομαι, περιέλαβον, embrace

πιστεύω, believe in, put one's trust or faith in (+ dat.)

πρεσβύτης, -ου, ὁ, old man

πρός (adv.), in reference to, w/ respect to

πτερόω, set on the wing, excite; (pass.) be excited

ῥόπαλον, τό, club, cudgel (used to beat donkeys/asses/mules)

σκοπέω, look at, consider, examine

σμίλη, ἡ, knife for carving/pruning

τε (particle/conj.), and

τε καί/τε...καί, (both)...and

τις, τι, (gen. τινος) (indef. adj.) a certain; some; a, an; (indef. pron.) someone; something; anyone; anything; neut. τι as adv., 'at all'; τις...τις, 'one (person)...another (person)...'

τίς, τί (gen. τίνος; interrog. pron. and adj.), who? which? what?

τολμάω, dare, be bold enough to (+ inf.)

ὑπό, (prep. + gen.) (w/ pass. voice) by

ὕπουλος, -ον, false, deceitful, deceptive, secretly hostile

φέρω, bear, bring

φημί, say

φρήν, φρενός, ἡ, heart, mind

χαίρω, rejoice, be glad or delighted

χείρ, χειρός/χερός (poetic), ἡ, hand; ἐκ χειρὸς/χερὸς, 'near at hand,' 'at close range'; w/ one's hand(s)

χρήζω, desire, long for (+ gen.)

ὡραῖος, -η, -ον, in the bloom of youth, beautiful

The Lion and the Old Man's Daughter - Continued
(Babrius 98 = Perry 140)

ἔκειτο δ' ἀργὸς ὥσπερ ὗς ἀποθνήσκων,

γέροντος ἀνδρὸς ποικίλου τε τὴν γνώμην

σοφίῃ διδαχθεὶς ὡς ἄμικτον ἀνθρώποις

20   ἐρᾶν λεόντων ἢ λέοντας ἀνθρώπων.

18-19   γέροντος...διδαχθεὶς = διδαχθεὶς σοφίῃ γέροντος τε ποικίλου ἀνδρὸς τὴν γνώμην

19   διδαχθεὶς masc. nom. sing. aor. pass. part. < διδάσκω
     ἄμικτον sc. ἐστί

20   λέοντας ἀνθρώπων to preserve the grammatical parallel, λέοντας should be dat. pl., i.e., λεόντεσσι /λείουσι (Epic), but the meter will not allow it. So in this case the first indir. statement is ὡς + indic. (ἐστί), while the second is acc. + inf.

L'Estrange (1692)

A *LYON* was in Love with a Country Lass, and desir'd her Father's Consent to have her in Marriage. The Answer he gave was churlish enough. He'd never agree to't he said, upon any Terms, to marry his Daughter to a Beast. The *Lyon* gave him a sour Look upon't, which brought the Bumpkin, upon second Thoughts, to strike a Bargain with him, upon these Conditions: that his Teeth should be drawn, and his Nails pair'd; for those were things, he said, that the foolish Girl was terribly afraid of. The *Lyon* sends for a Surgeon immediately to do the Work; (as what will not Love make a body do?) and so soon as ever the Operation was over, he goes and challenges the Father upon his Promise. The Countryman seeing the *Lyon* disarm'd, pluck'd up a good Heart, and with a swinging Cudgel so order'd the matter, that he brake off the Match.

THE MORAL. *An extravagant Love, consults neither Life, Fortune, nor Reputation, but sacrifices all that can be dear to a Man of Sense and Honour, to the transports of an inconsiderate Passion.*

ἄμικτος, -ον, incompatible

ἀνήρ, ἀνδρός, ὁ, man

ἄνθρωπος, ὁ, man, human being

ἀποθνῄσκω, die

ἀργός, -ή, -όν, inactive, sluggish; useless

γέρων, -οντος, ὁ, old man; (as adj., mostly w/ masc. noun) old

γνώμη, ἡ, (moral) maxim

διδάσκω, teach

ἐράω, love, be in love w/ (+ gen.)

ἤ (conj.), or

κεῖμαι, lie

ποικίλος, -η, -ον, subtle, wily

σοφία/σοφίη (Epic/Ionic), ἡ, cleverness; intelligence; wisdom

τε (particle/conj.), and

ὗς/ὕν, ὑός, ὁ/ἡ, pig, boar

ὡς (conj.; = ὅτι), that

ὥσπερ (adv.), just as, like

Linton (1887)

Though the Lion in love let them draw
All his teeth, and pare down every claw,
He'd no bride for his pains,
For they beat out his brains
Ere he set on his maiden a paw.

OUR VERY MEANS MAY DEFEAT OUR ENDS

[For illustration, see back cover.]

Jacobs (1894)

A Lion once fell in love with a beautiful maiden and proposed marriage to her parents. The old people did not know what to say. They did not like to give their daughter to the Lion, yet they did not wish to enrage the King of Beasts. At last the father said: "We feel highly honoured by your Majesty's proposal, but you see our daughter is a tender young thing, and we fear that in the vehemence of your affection you might possibly do her some injury. Might I venture to suggest that your Majesty should have your claws removed, and your teeth extracted, then we would gladly consider your proposal again." The Lion was so much in love that he had his claws trimmed and his big teeth taken out. But when he came again to the parents of the young girl they simply laughed in his face, and bade him do his worst.

Love can tame the wildest.

27. The Two Friends and the Bear
(Chambry 255/254 = Perry 65)

Δύο φίλοι τὴν αὐτὴν ὁδὸν ἐβάδιζον. Ἄρκτου δὲ αὐτοῖς ἐπιφανείσης, ὁ μὲν ἕτερος φθάσας ἀνέβη ἐπί τι δένδρον καὶ ἐνταῦθα ἐκρύπτετο, ὁ δὲ ἕτερος μέλλων περικατάληπτος γίνεσθαι, πεσὼν κατὰ τοῦ ἐδάφους τὸν νεκρὸν

5   προσεποιεῖτο. Τῆς δὲ ἄρκτου προσενεγκούσης αὐτῷ τὸ ῥύγχος καὶ περιοσφραινομένης τὰς ἀναπνοὰς συνεῖχε· φασὶ γὰρ νεκροῦ μὴ ἅπτεσθαι τὸ ζῷον. Ἀπαλλαγείσης δέ, ὁ ἀπὸ τοῦ δένδρου καταβὰς ἐπυνθάνετο αὐτοῦ τί ἡ ἄρκτος πρὸς τὸ οὖς εἴρηκεν. Ὁ δὲ εἶπε· "Τοῦ λοιποῦ τοιούτοις μὴ

10 συνοδοιπορεῖν φίλοις οἳ ἐν κινδύνοις οὐ παραμένουσιν."

Ὁ λόγος δηλοῖ ὅτι τοὺς γνησίους τῶν φίλων αἱ συμφοραὶ δοκιμάζουσιν.

---

1 τὴν αὐτὴν in the attributive position, αὐτός, -ή, -ό = 'the same'
1-2 Ἄρκτου...ἐπιφανείσης gen. abs.
2 ἐπιφανείσης fem. gen. sing. aor. pass. part. < ἐπιφαίνω
φθάσας ἀνέβη i.e., before his friend (and apparently the tree only had room for one person)
5-6 Τῆς...ἄρκτου προσενεγκούσης...περιοσφραινομένης gen. abs. x2
6-7 φασὶ...ζῷον = γὰρ φασὶ τὸ ζῷον μὴ ἅπτεσθαι νεκροῦ
7 μὴ Cl. Gk. would use οὐ w/ inf. in indir. statement after verbs of saying and thinking, but will substitute μή "in emphatic declarations and expressions of thought which involve a wish that the utterance may hold good" (Smyth § 2723). This, however, does not seem to be one of those cases, and may simply be a L. Gk. substitution of μή for οὐ
Ἀπαλλαγείσης sc. ἄρκτου; gen. abs.
Ἀπαλλαγείσης fem. gen. sing. aor. pass. part. < ἀπαλλάσσω.
8 καταβὰς masc. nom. sing. aor. act. part. < καταβαίνω
9 εἴρηκεν 3rd sing. perf. act. indic. < λέγω
9-10 συνοδοιπορεῖν inf. may be used for 2nd pers. impera. "This infinitive is commoner in poetry than in prose (where it has a solemn or formal force)." (Smyth § 2013)
11 τοὺς γνησίους τῶν φίλων lit., 'the genuine/true friends of (one's) friends,' i.e., who your real friends are

ἀναβαίνω, ἀναβήσομαι, ἀνέβην, go up, climb

ἀναπνοή, ἡ, breath, breathing

ἀπαλλάσσω, set free, release; (pass.) stop what one is doing and leave/depart

ἅπτω, fasten; (mid.) lay hold of or touch X (gen.); attack X (gen.)

ἄρκτος, ἡ, bear

αὐτός, -ή, -ό, (pron. in gen., dat., acc.) him, her, it; them; (adj.) same

βαδίζω, go; + ὁδὸν, travel (on) a road

γί(γ)νομαι, be

γνήσιος, ὁ, genuine, true or real friend

δένδρον, τό, tree

δηλόω, show, reveal

δοκιμάζω, put to the test, make trial of, prove

δύο (indecl.), two

ἔδαφος, -εος/ους, τό, ground

ἐνταῦθα (adv.), there

ἐπί (prep. + acc.), onto, up onto

ἐπιφαίνω, show forth; (pass.) come (suddenly) into view, appear

ἕτερος, -η, -ον, other, another; (usu. w/ article) the other (one of two)

ζῷον/ζῶον, τό, animal

κατά (prep. + gen.), down to/upon

καταβαίνω, go or come down

κίνδυνος, ὁ, danger

κρύπτω, hide, conceal

λέγω, λέξω/ἐρῶ, εἶπον, say

λόγος, ὁ, story, tale

λοιπός, -ή, -όν, remaining; τοῦ λοιποῦ, henceforward, hereafter, from this point on

μέλλω, be about to (+ pres. or fut. inf.)

νεκρός, ὁ, dead body, corpse

ὅτι (conj.), that

οὖς, ὠτός, τό, ear

παραμένω, stay beside or w/ (one), remain by (one's side), stand close by (one)

περικατάληπτος, -ον, overtaken, caught

περιοσφραίνομαι, smell or sniff around

πίπτω, πεσοῦμαι, ἔπεσον, throw oneself down, fall down

προσποιέω, make over to; (mid.) pretend to be X (acc.)

προσφέρω, προσοίσω, προσήνεγκον, bring (to)

πυνθάνομαι, inquire (of), ask (+ gen.)

ῥύγχος, -εος, τό, snout

συμφορά, ἡ, misfortune, bad luck, disaster

συνέχω, hold

συνοδοιπορέω, journey or travel together w/ (+ dat.)

τις, τι, (gen. τινος) (indef. adj.) a certain; some; a, an; any; (indef. pron.) someone; something; anyone; anything

τίς, τί (gen. τίνος; interrog. pron. and adj.), who? which? what?

τοιοῦτος, -αύτη, -οῦτο, such as this; (frequently w/ implication based on context) so good/bad/etc. ...as this

φημί, say

φθάνω, φθήσομαι, ἔφθασα, come to before; aor. part. φθάς/φθάσας is used like an adv. w/ meaning 'before,' 'first'

φίλος, -η, -ον, dear, beloved; (as substantive) friend

28. The Father, the Son, and the Lion
(Chambry 296 [Variant 1] = Perry 363)

Υἱόν τις γέρων δειλὸς μονογενῆ ἔχων γενναῖον,
κυνηγεῖν ἐφιέμενον, εἶδε τοῦτον καθ᾽ ὕπνους ὑπὸ λέοντος
ἀναλωθέντα. Φοβηθεὶς δὲ μή πως ὁ ὄνειρος ἀληθεύσῃ,
οἴκημα κάλλιστον καὶ μετέωρον κατεσκεύασε, κἀκεῖσε τὸν
5   υἱὸν εἰσαγαγὼν ἐφύλαττεν. Ἐζωγράφησε δὲ ἐν τῷ οἰκήματι
πρὸς τέρψιν τοῦ υἱοῦ παντοῖα ζῷα, ἐν οἷς ἦν καὶ λέων. Ὁ δὲ
ταῦτα μᾶλλον ὁρῶν πλείονα λύπην εἶχε. Καὶ δήποτε
πλησίον τοῦ λέοντος στὰς εἶπεν· "Ὦ κάκιστον θηρίον, διὰ
σὲ καὶ τὸν ψευδῆ ὄνειρον τοῦ ἐμοῦ πατρὸς τῇδε τῇ οἰκίᾳ
10   κατεκλείσθην, ὡς ἐν φρουρᾷ· τί σοι ποιήσω;"

[Continued on page 100]

---

3   **ἀναλωθέντα** masc. nom. sing. aor. pass. part. < ἀναλίσκω
4   **κἀκεῖσε** = καὶ + ἐκεῖσε
8   **στὰς** masc. nom. sing. aor. act. part. < ἵστημι
10   **κατεκλείσθην** 1st sing. aor. pass. indic. < κατακλείω
ποιήσω < ποιέω/ποιῶ; either 1st sing. aor. act. subju. (deliberative) or 1st sing. fut. act. indic.

ἀληθεύω, prove or come true

ἀναλίσκω/ἀναλόω, ἀναλώσω, ἀνήλωσα, kill, destroy

γενναῖος, -α, -ον, high-minded, high-spirited; intense

γέρων, -οντος, ὁ, old man

δειλός, -ή, -όν, cowardly

δήποτε/δή ποτε (particle), indeed one time

διά (prep. + acc.), because of

εἰσάγω, εἰσάξω, εἰσήγαγον, lead in

ἐκεῖσε (adv.), there, in that place

ἐμός, -ή, -όν, my

ἐφίημι, incite; (mid.) desire to (+ inf.)

ζωγραφέω, paint

ζῷον/ζῶον, τό, animal, creature

θηρίον, τό, wild animal, (savage) beast

ἵστημι, make X stand; stop X; set X (up); (2nd aor.; perf.) stand

κακός, -ή, -όν, evil, wicked, bad

καλός, -ή, -όν, beautiful

κατακλείω, shut in; (pass.) be shut up in X (dat.)

κατασκευάζω, build, construct

κυνηγέω, hunt, go hunting

λέγω, λέξω/ἐρῶ, εἶπον, say

λέων, -οντος, ὁ, lion

λύπη, ἡ, mental pain, grief, anguish

μᾶλλον (adv.), more and more

μετέωρος, -ον, raised from off the ground, suspended in the air

μήπως/μή πως (adv.; often after vbs. of fearing), if by chance, if possibly (+ subju.)

μονογενής, -ές, only, only-begotten

ὅδε, ἥδε, τόδε, this; (pl.) these

οἴκημα, -ατος, τό, house

οἰκία, ἡ, house

ὄνειρος, ὁ, dream

ὁρῶ, ὄψομαι, εἶδον, see

ὅς, ἥ, ὅ (rel. pron.), who, whose, whom, which, that

οὗτος, αὕτη, τοῦτο, this; (pl.) these

παντοῖος, -η, -ον, all sorts/kinds of

πατήρ, πατρός, ὁ, father

πλείων, πλεῖον, -ονος (gen.), greater

πλησίον (adv./prep. + gen.), near

ποιέω/ποιῶ, do

πρός (prep. + acc.), for

τέρψις, -εως, ἡ, delight, enjoyment

τις, τι, (gen. τινος) (indef. adj.) a certain; some; a, an; (indef. pron.) someone; something; anyone; anything

τίς, τί (gen. τίνος; interrog. pron. and adj.), who? which? what?

υἱός, ὁ, son

ὕπνος, ὁ, sleep (sing. and pl. often interchangeable); κατὰ (τοὺς) ὕπνους, in sleep, in a dream

ὑπό, (prep. + gen.) (w/ pass. voice) by

φοβέομαι/φοβοῦμαι, fear, be afraid

φρουρά, ἡ, prison

φυλάττω, guard, watch, keep a watch on, keep (in a place)

ψευδής, -ές, lying, false

ὡς (conj.), as, just as

The Father, the Son, and the Lion - Continued
(Chambry 296 [Variant 1] = Perry 363)

10   Καὶ εἰπὼν ἐπέβαλε τῷ

τοίχῳ τὴν χεῖρα ἐκτυφλῶσαι τὸν λέοντα. Σκόλοψ δὲ τῷ

δακτύλῳ αὐτοῦ ἐμπαρεὶς ὄγκωμα καὶ φλεγμονὴν μέχρι

βουβῶνος εἰργάσατο· πυρετὸς δὲ ἐπιγενόμενος αὐτῷ θᾶττον

τοῦ βίου μετέστησεν. Ὁ δὲ λέων καὶ οὕτως ἀνήρηκε τὸν

15 παῖδα, μηδὲν τῷ τοῦ πατρὸς ὠφεληθέντα σοφίσματι.

     Ὁ μῦθος δηλοῖ ὅτι οὐδεὶς δύναται τὸ μέλλον ἐκφυγεῖν.

---

11   ἐκτυφλῶσαι inf. of purpose (Smyth § 2008)
12   ἐμπαρεὶς masc. nom. sing. aor. pass. part. < ἐμπείρω
14   μετέστησεν 3rd sing. 2nd aor. act. indic. < μεθίστημι
         καὶ οὕτως when joined w/ an adv., καί gives emphasis, i.e., 'in this very manner,' 'thus, in fact'
         ἀνήρηκε 3rd sing. perf. act. indic. < ἀναιρέω
15   ὠφεληθέντα masc. acc. sing. aor. pass. part. < ὠφελέω

William Mulready (1807)

ἀναιρέω, destroy, kill

αὐτός, -ή, -ό, (pron. in gen., dat., acc.) him, her, it; them

βίος, ὁ, life

βουβών, -ῶνος, ὁ, groin

δάκτυλος, ὁ, finger

δηλόω, show, reveal

δύναμαι, be able or strong enough to (+ inf.)

ἐκτυφλόω, blind, make (quite) blind

ἐκφεύγω, ἐκφεύξομαι, ἐκέφυγον, escape (completely), (utterly) escape

ἐμπείρω, (act. is rare) fasten onto; (pass. here w. reflex. sense) fasten itself to, pierce (+ dat.)

ἐπιβάλλω, ἐπιβαλῶ, ἐπέβαλον, throw X (acc.) on/against Y (dat.)

ἐπιγί(γ)νομαι, ἐπιγενήσομαι, ἐπεγενόμην, come upon, attack (+ dat.)

ἐργάζομαι, ἐργάσομαι, εἰργασάμην, cause

θᾶττον (adv.), rather swiftly/quickly

μεθίστημι, change; set free (1st aor. pass; 2nd aor. act., perf. act., pluperf. act.) cease from (+ gen.); + βίου, die

μέλλω, be destined/going to (happen)

μέχρι (prep. + gen.), even to, as far as

μηδέν (adv.), not at all, in no way

μῦθος, ὁ, story, fable, tale

ὄγκωμα, -ατος, τό, swelling

ὅτι (conj.), that

οὐδείς, οὐδεμία, οὐδέν, no one, nothing, no

οὕτως (adv.), in this way, thus

παῖς, παιδός, ὁ/ἡ, child

πυρετός, τό, fever

σκόλοψ, -οπος, ὁ, splinter

σόφισμα, -ατος, τό, ingenious contrivance, clever plan

τοῖχος, ὁ, wall (of a house)

φλεγμονή, ἡ, inflammation

χείρ, χειρός, ἡ, hand

ὠφελέω, help; (pass.) be helped by (+ dat.)

29. The Father, the Son, and the Lion
(Babrius 136 = Perry 363)

Υἱὸν μονογενῆ δειλὸς εἶχε πρεσβύτης
γενναῖον ἄλλως καὶ θέλοντα θηρεύειν.
τοῦτον καθ' ὕπνους ὑπὸ λέοντος ᾠήθη
θανόντα κεῖσθαι· καὶ φοβούμενος μήπως
5   ὕπαρ γένηται καὶ τὸ φάσμ' ἀληθεύσῃ,
κάλλιστον οἶκον ἐξελέξατ' ἀνδρῶνα,
ὑψηλὸν, εὐδμητὸν τε χηλίου πλήρη,
κἀκεῖ τὸν υἱὸν παρεφύλασσε συγκλείσας.
χὥπως ἔχῃ τι βουκόλημα τῆς λύπης
10   ἐνέθηκε τοίχοις ποικίλας γραφὰς ζῴων,
ἐν οἷς ἅπασι καὶ λέων ἐμορφώθη.
ὁρῶντα δ' αὐτὸν μᾶλλον εἶχεν ἡ λύπη
καὶ δή ποθ' ἑστὼς τοῦ λέοντος οὐ πόρρω
"κάκιστε θηρῶν" εἶπεν "ὡς σὺ τὸν ψεύστην
15   ὄνειρον ἄλλως ὄμμασιν πατρὸς δείξας
ἔχεις με φρουρῇ περιβαλὼν γυναικείῃ.

[Continued on page 104]

3-4 τοῦτον...κεῖσθαι = ᾠήθη καθ' ὕπνους τοῦτον κεῖσθαι θανόντα ὑπὸ
λέοντος

6 ἀνδρῶνα in apposition to κάλλιστον οἶκον, i.e., he chose a home that was
only to be used by the men of the family

7 χηλίου = καὶ + ἡλίου

8 κἀκεῖ = καὶ + ἐκεῖ

9 χὥπως = καὶ + ὅπως

13 ἑστὼς masc. nom. sing. perf. act. part. < ἵστημι

14 κάκιστε masc. voc. sing. superl. < κακός, -ή, -όν

16 γυναικείῃ either adj. modifying φρουρῇ or noun in apposition to it

ἀληθεύω, prove or come true

ἄλλως (adv.), (+ substantive) pure and simple, no other than; ἄλλως (τε) καὶ, especially and

ἀνδρών, -ῶνος, ὁ, men's quarters in a house

ἅπας, ἅπασα, ἅπαν, all

βουκόλημα, -ατος, τό, alleviation or distraction from (+ gen.)

γενναῖος, -α, -ον, high-minded, high-spirited; intense

γί(γ)νομαι, come about, occur, happen

γραφή, ἡ, painting

γυναικεῖος, -α, -ον, fit for women; (as substantive) ἡ γυναικεία, women's quarters in a house

δείκνυμι, δείξω, ἔδειξα, show, exhibit

δειλός, -ή, -όν, cowardly

δή (particle), in truth, indeed

ἐκεῖ (adv.), there, in that place

ἐκλέγω, pick out; (mid.) pick out for oneself, choose

ἐντίθημι, ἐνθήσω, ἐνέθηκα, put X (acc.) on Y (dat.)

εὔδμητος, -όν, well-built

ἔχω, have, hold, keep; enclose; (+ aor. part. = auxiliary vb. giving a perf. sense)

ζῷον/ζῶον, τό, animal, creature

ἥλιος, ὁ, sun, sunlight

θέλω, be inclined by nature, want (+ inf.)

θήρ, θηρός, ὁ, beast of prey (esp. of a lion), wild beast

θηρεύω, hunt, go hunting

θνήσκω, θανοῦμαι, ἔθανον, die; (2nd aor.; perf.) be dead

ἵστημι, make X stand; stop X; set X (up); (2nd aor.; perf.) stand

κακός, -ή, -όν, evil, wicked, bad

καλός, -ή, -όν, beautiful

κεῖμαι, lie

λέων, -οντος, ὁ, lion

λύπη, ἡ, sad condition; mental pain, grief

μᾶλλον (adv.), more, still more

μήπως (adv.; often after vbs. of fearing), lest perchance/possibly (+ subju.)

μονογενής, -ές, only, only-begotten

μορφόω, give form; (pass.) take on a form, be formed/painted

οἶκος, ὁ, house

οἴομαι, οἰήσομαι, ᾠήθην, imagine

ὄμμα, -ατος, τό, eye

ὄνειρος, ὁ, dream

ὅπως (conj.), so that, in order that (+ subju.)

ὁρῶ, ὄψομαι, εἶδον, see

ὅς, ἥ, ὅ (rel. pron.), who, whose, whom, which, that

οὗτος, αὕτη, τοῦτο, this; (pl.) these

παῖς, παιδός, ὁ/ἡ, child

παραφυλάσσω, guard closely, watch carefully

πατήρ, πατρός, ὁ, father

περιβάλλω, περιβαλῶ, περέβαλον, surround w/ (+ dat.)

πλήρης, -ες, full of (+ gen.)

ποικίλος, -η, -ον, various, diverse; richly colored

πόρρω (adv.), far from (+ gen.)

ποτε (adv.), at one time, once

πρεσβύτης, -ου, ὁ, old man

συγκλείω, shut in

τις, τι, (gen. τινος) (indef. adj.) a certain; some; a, an; (indef. pron.) someone; something; anyone; anything

τοῖχος, ὁ, wall (of a house)

υἱός, ὁ, son

ὕπαρ (adv.), really, actually

ὕπνος, ὁ, sleep (sing. and pl. often interchangeable); κατὰ (τοὺς) ὕπνους, in sleep, in a dream

ὑπό, (prep. + gen.) by, at the hands of

ὑψηλός, -ή, -όν, high, lofty

φάσμα, -ατος, τό, apparition, portent, omen

φοβέομαι/φοβοῦμαι, fear, be afraid

φρουρά/φρουρή (Ionic), ἡ, prison

ψεύστης, -ου, ὁ, liar, cheat; (as adj.) lying, false

ὡς (conj.), since, because

The Father, the Son, and the Lion - Continued
(Babrius 136 = Perry 363)

τί δὴ 'πὶ σοὶ λόγοισιν εἶμι κοὐκ ἔργον

ποιῶ βίαιον;" τῷ δὲ φρουρίου τοίχῳ

ἐπέβαλε χεῖρας τὸν λέοντα τυφλώσων,

20   σκόλοψ ἀποσχισθεὶς δὲ τοῦ ξύλου τούτῳ

ἔδυν' ὑπ' ὄνυχα, χὠ πατὴρ καθαιμώδους

φλογώσεως τὰς σάρκας εὐθὺς εἰσδύσης

ἅπαντα ποιῶν ἤνυσ' οὐδὲν ὁ τλήμων·

θέρμη δ' ἐπ' αὐτοῖς υἱὸν ἄχρι βουβώνων

25   ἀνῆψεν ὥστε τὸν βίον τελευτῆσαι.

ὁ πρέσβυς οὕτως οὐκ ἔσωσε τὸν παῖδα

μέλλοντα θνήσκειν ὑπὸ λέοντος ἀψύχου.

Ἃ σοι πέπρωται ταῦτα τλῆθι γενναίως

καὶ μὴ σοφίζου· τὸ χρεὼν γὰρ οὐ φεύξῃ.

---

17   λόγοισιν instrumental dat. (Smyth § 1503). This line contains a famous dichotomy in ancient Greek thought known as the *logos-ergon* contrast between mere 'words' and actual 'deeds'
εἶμι here pres. tense; in Attic prose εἶμι (usu.) serves as fut. of ἔρχομαι
κοὐκ = καὶ + οὐκ

19   τυφλώσων fut. part. expresses purpose (Smyth § 2065)

20   ἀποσχισθεὶς masc. nom. sing. aor. pass. part. < ἀποσχίζω
τοῦ ξύλου ancient paintings were painted on wood panels, not canvas
τούτῳ dat. of disadvantage (Smyth § 1481), often best translated into English by a possessive gen.

21   χὠ = καὶ + ὁ
καθαιμώδους φλογώσεως...εἰσδύσης gen. abs.

24   ἐπ' αὐτοῖς the pron. precedes the noun (βουβώνων), conveying how quickly the fever spread

28   Ἃ σοι πέπρωται ταῦτα = ταῦτα ἅ πέπρωται σοι. In Gk., the rel. pron. can precede its antecedent (this occurs more often in verse than in prose). The entire phrase is the obj. of τλῆθι
τλῆθι 2nd sing. aor. act. impera. < τλάω

29   σοφίζου 2nd sing. pres. mid/pass. (dep.). impera. < σοφίζομαι

ἀνάπτω, ἀνάψω, ἀνῆψα, fasten upon; attack; consume w/ fever

ἀνύω, achieve, accomplish

ἀποσχίζω, sever or detach from; (pass.) be detached from (+ gen.)

αὐτός, -ή, -ό, (pron. in gen., dat., acc.) him, her, it; them

ἄχρι (prep. + gen.), even to, as far as

ἄψυχος, -ον, lifeless, inanimate

βίαιος, -α, -ον, violent

βίος, ὁ, life

βουβών, -ῶνος, ὁ, (sing./pl.) groin

γενναίως (adv.), nobly

δύω/δύνω, δύσομαι, ἔδυνα, enter, get into; plunge in

εἰσδύνω, εἰσδύσομαι, εἰσέδυν, go into, enter

εἶμι, go

ἐπί (prep. + dat.), against; on

ἐπιβάλλω, ἐπιβαλῶ, ἐπέβαλον, throw X (acc.) on/against Y (dat.)

ἔργον, τό, deed

εὐθύς (adv.), at once, immediately

θέρμη, ἡ, feverish heat

καθαιμώδης, -ες, bloody

λόγος, ὁ, word

μέλλω, be destined to (usu. + fut. inf.; rarely w/ pres. inf.)

ξύλον, τό, wood

ὄνυξ, -υχος, ὁ, nail

οὐδείς, οὐδεμία, οὐδέν, no one, nothing, no

οὕτω/οὕτως (adv.), in this way, thus

πέπρωται, (usu. 3rd sing. perf. only) it has been/is fated, allotted, or foredoomed

ποιέω/ποιῶ, do

πρέσβυς, -εως/εος, ὁ, old man

σάρξ, σαρκός, ἡ, flesh; (pl.) flesh (of the body), body

σκόλοψ, -οπος, ὁ, splinter

σοφίζομαι, evade through one's use of clever tricks or contrivances

σώζω, save (from death), keep alive

τε (particle/conj.), and

τελευτάω, complete, finish; + βίον, die

τίς, τί (gen. τίνος; interrog. pron. and adj.), who? which? what?; τί, 'why'?

τλάω, τλήσομαι, ἔτλην, bear, submit to, endure

τλήμων, -ονος, ὁ/ἡ, suffering, wretched or miserable person

τυφλόω, blind, make blind

ὑπό (prep. + gen.), by, at the hands of; (prep. + acc.), under

φεύγω, φεύξομαι, ἔφυγον, escape

φλόγωσις, -εως, ἡ, inflammation

φρούριον, τό, prison

χείρ, χειρός, ἡ, hand

χρεών, τό (indecl.), that which must be, necessity, fate

ὥστε (conj. + inf.), w/ the result that

30. The Ant and the Cicada
(Syntipas 43 = Perry 373)

Μύρμηξ τις ὥρᾳ χειμῶνος ὃν θέρους συνήγαγε σῖτον καθ᾽
ἑαυτὸν ἤσθιεν. ὁ δὲ τέττιξ προσελθὼν αὐτῷ ἠτεῖτο
μεταδοθῆναι αὐτῷ ἐκ τῶν αὐτοῦ σιτίων. ὁ δὲ μύρμηξ ἔφη
πρὸς αὐτόν "καὶ τί ἄρα πράττων διετέλεις ἐφ᾽ ὅλῳ τῷ τοῦ
5 θέρους καιρῷ, ὅτι μὴ συνέλεξας σῖτον ἑαυτῷ εἰς διατροφήν;"
ὁ δὲ τέττιξ ἀντέφησεν αὐτῷ ὡς "τῷ μελῳδεῖν
ἀπασχολούμενος τῆς συλλογῆς ἐκωλυόμην." τῇ γοῦν τοιαύτῃ
τοῦ τέττιγος ἀποκρίσει ὁ μύρμηξ ἐπιγελάσας, τὸν ἑαυτοῦ
σῖτον τοῖς ἐνδοτέροις τῆς γῆς μυχοῖς ἐναπέκρυψε καὶ πρὸς
10 αὐτὸν ἀπεφθέγξατο ὡς "ἐπεὶ τότε ματαίως ἐμελῴδεις, νυνὶ
λοιπὸν ὀρχήσασθαι θέλησον."

Οὗτος παρίστησι τοὺς ὀκνηρούς τε καὶ ἀμελεῖς, καὶ τοὺς
ἐν ματαιοπραγματίαις διάγοντας κἀντεῦθεν ὑστερουμένους.

---

1 **ὥρᾳ** dat. of time when (Smyth § 1540)

1-2 **ὃν...ἤσθιεν** = ἤσθιεν σῖτον ὃν συνήγαγε καθ᾽ ἑαυτὸν θέρους

1 **θέρους** gen. of time within which (Smyth § 1444)
   καθ᾽ = κατὰ

2 **τέττιξ** the onomatopoeic name of a winged insect (a kind of cicada or grasshopper) fond of basking in trees. The male makes a chirping or clicking noise ('tet-tix') by means of certain drums or 'tymbals' underneath its wings

3 **μεταδοθῆναι** aor. pass. inf. < μεταδίδωμι

4 **ἐφ᾽** = ἐπὶ

4-5 **τῷ...καιρῷ** dat. of time when (Smyth § 1540)

5 **μὴ** Cl. Gk. would use οὐ

6 **τῷ μελῳδεῖν** articular inf. (lit. 'in/with singing') governed by ἀπασχολούμενος

7-8 **τῇ...ἀποκρίσει** note separation of article from noun, w/ modifying particle (γοῦν), adj. (τοιαύτῃ), and gen. of possession (τοῦ τέττιγος) in between, thus making the entire phrase especially emphatic

11 **θέλησον** 2nd sing. aor. act. impera. < ἐθέλω/θέλω

12 **Οὗτος** = Οὗτος μῦθος/λόγος

13 **τοὺς ἐν ματαιοπραγματίαις διάγοντας** substantive noun phrase
    κἀντεῦθεν crasis of καὶ + ἐντεῦθεν

αἰτέω, ask, beg

ἀμελής, -ές, careless, negligent

ἀντίφημι, ἀντίφήσω, ἀντέφησα, answer, reply

ἀπασχολέω, leave one no leisure; (pass.) be wholly occupied or engrossed in something (dat.) so as to attend to nothing else

ἀπόκρισις, -εως, ἡ, answer

ἀποφθέγγομαι, speak one's opinion plainly; utter an apophthegm

ἄρα (particle), after all; therefore, then

αὐτός, -ή, -ό, (pron. in gen., dat., acc.) him, her, it; them

γῆ, ἡ, earth, ground

γοῦν (particle), οὖν ('then') + γε (here putting emphasis on the word that follows instead of, as normally, on the preceding word; this is because the word that precedes it is an article)

διάγω, spend one's life

διατελέω, accomplish; be X-ing (part.) all along

διατροφή, ἡ, sustenance and support

ἑαυτοῦ, ἑαυτῆς, ἑαυτοῦ, (refl. pron. in gen., dat., acc.) himself, herself, itself

ἐθέλω/θέλω, be willing (+ inf.)

εἰς (prep. + acc.), for

ἐναποκρύπτω, hide from in, hide from sight in, conceal in (+ dat.)

ἐνδότερος, ον, inner

ἐντεῦθεν (adv.), therefore, as a result

ἐπεί (conj.), since

ἐπί (prep. + dat.), in [the time of], during

ἐπιγελάω, laugh at (+ dat.)

ἐσθίω, eat

θέρος, θέρους, τό, summer; harvest

καιρός, ὁ, critical time; time, season

κατά (prep. + acc.), by

κωλύω, hinder, prevent; (pass.) be hindered or prevented from (+ gen.)

λοιπόν (adv.), from now on, henceforth

ματαιοπραγματεία, ἡ, foolish pursuit or pastime

ματαίως (adv.), foolishly

μελῳδέω, sing

μεταδίδωμι, give a part of, give a share

μύρμηξ, -ηκος, ὁ, ant

μυχός, ὁ, innermost part, nook, recess, store chamber

νυνί (adv.; strengthened form of νῦν), now

ὅλος, -η, -ον, entire, whole

ὀκνηρός, -ά, -όν, idle, sluggish

ὀρχέομαι, dance

ὅς, ἥ, ὅ (rel. pron.), who, whose, whom, which, that

ὅτι (conj.), that

οὗτος, αὕτη, τοῦτο, this; (pl.) these

παρίστημι, show, depict

πράττω, have to do, be busy with

προσέρχομαι, πρόσειμι, προσῆλθον, come or go to (+ dat.)

σιτίον, τό, grain, wheat; (mostly in pl.) provisions, victuals, food

σῖτος, ὁ, grain, food

συλλέγω, gather, collect

συλλογή, ἡ, gathering, collecting

συνάγω, συνάξω, συνήγαγον, gather together (stores, crops, etc.)

τε καί/τε...καί, (both)...and

τέττιξ, -ιγος ὁ, tettix, cicada

τις, τι, (gen. τινος) (indef. adj.) a certain; some; a, an

τίς, τί (gen. τίνος; interrog. pron. and adj.), who? which? what?

τοιοῦτος, -αύτη, -οῦτο, such as this; (frequently w/ implication based on context) so good/bad/etc. ...as this

τότε (adv.), then, at that time

ὑστερέω, come too late; (mid.) be in want, lack, be in straightened circumstances; be worse off

φημί, φήσω, ἔφην, say

χειμών, -ῶνος, ὁ, winter; χειμῶνος ὥρᾳ, in winter, in wintertime

ὥρα, ἡ, season

ὡς (= ὅτι), often introduces a quotation in dir. disc. and should not be translated

Goldsmith (1784)

'Twas that bleak season of the year,
In which no smiles, no charms appear;
Bare were the trees; the rivers froze;
The hills and mountains capt with snows;
When, lodging scarce and victuals scant,
A Grasshopper address'd an Ant:
And, in a supplicating tone,
Begg'd he would make her case his own.

   "It was, indeed, a bitter task
To those who were used to ask;
Yet she was forc'd the truth to say,
She had not broke her fast that day;
His worship, tho', with plenty bless'd,
Knew how to pity the distress'd;
A grain of corn to her was gold,
And Heav'n would yield him fifty-fold."

   The Ant beheld her wretched plight,
Nor seem'd unfeeling at the sight;
Yet, still inquisitive to know
How she became reduc'd so low,
Asked her – we'll e'en suppose in rhyme –
What she did all the summer time?

   "In summer time, good sir," said she,
"Ah! these were merry months with me!
I thought of nothing but delight,
And sung, Lord, help me! day and night:
Through yonder meadows did you pass,
You must have heard me in the grass."

   "Ah!" cry'd the Ant, and knit his brow –
"But 'tis enough I hear you now;
And, Madam Songstress, to be plain,
You seek my charity in vain:
What, shall th' industrious yield his due
To thriftless vagabonds like you!
Some corn I have, but none to spare,
Next summer learn to take more care;
And in your frolic moods, remember,
July is follow'd by December."

La Fontaine (1668)

(trans. Hill [2008])

The Cicada, having sung
All summer long,
Was in want and starving thin
Once the winter wind set in.
With no slightest scrap put by,
Bit of worm or bit of fly,
She approached her neighbor, Ant,
Pleading for a loan, a scant
Seed or two to live upon,
Just till these hard times had gone.
She'd repay, no need to dun her,
Swore upon her insect's honor,
Principal and interest both.
But the ant to lend was loath:
Stinginess was her least blot.
"What did you do when it was hot?"
She asked the one who begged for aid.
"Please you, ma'am, I did the thing
I liked the best, which was to sing
Night and day at any chance."
"You sang, you say? Well, you have made
My answer easy – now, go dance!"

Arthur Rackham (1912)

Takeo Takei (1925)

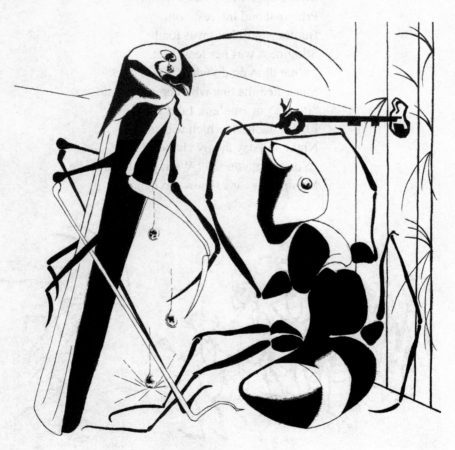

Jacob Lawrence (1970)

110

Gustave Doré (1867)

Allegorical Insects, Be Gone!

In Doré's illustration of La Fontaine's version of Aesop's fable, a female musician stands at a door in the snow with the children of the house looking up at her: the little girl with curiosity and, perhaps, sympathy (she does, after all, understand the pleasures of 'play' – note her doll and toy cart); her older brother, however, has a more ambiguous gaze, possibly mixing sympathy with a more judgmental streak (note too that he, like his mother, and unlike his sister and the musician, has his head covered). Their mother, both literally and figuratively, looks down at the musician from the top of the steps. Her tireless industry is indicated by the fact that she continues knitting (even her scissors, dangling from a ribbon at her knees, are kept ready at hand at all times). Doré, however, unlike Aesop and La Fontaine, holds out a glimmer of hope for the 'musician/grasshopper' – the broom and log with an ax lodged in it just outside the house may suggest the future possibility of the musician working for food and/or shelter.

31. Aphrodite and the Weasel
(Chambry 76/76 = Perry 50)

Γαλῆ ἐρασθεῖσα νεανίσκου εὐπρέπους ηὔξατο τῇ
Ἀφροδίτῃ ὅπως αὐτὴν μεταμορφώσῃ εἰς γυναῖκά. Καὶ ἡ θεὸς
ἐλεήσασα αὐτῆς τὸ πάθος μετετύπωσεν αὐτὴν εἰς κόρην
εὐειδῆ, καὶ οὕτως ὁ νεανίσκος θεασάμενος αὐτὴν καὶ ἐρασθεὶς
5 οἴκαδε ὡς ἑαυτὸν ἀπήγαγε. Καθημένων δὲ αὐτῶν ἐν τῷ
θαλάμῳ, ἡ Ἀφροδίτη γνῶναι βουλομένη εἰ μεταβαλοῦσα τὸ
σῶμα ἡ γαλῆ καὶ τὸν τρόπον ἤλλαξε, μῦν εἰς τὸ μέσον
καθῆκεν. Ἡ δὲ ἐπιλαθομένη τῶν παρόντων ἐξαναστᾶσα ἀπὸ
τῆς κοίτης τὸν μῦν ἐδίωκε καταφαγεῖν θέλουσα. Καὶ ἡ θεὸς
10 ἀγανακτήσασα κατ' αὐτῆς πάλιν αὐτὴν εἰς τὴν ἀρχαίαν
φύσιν ἀποκατέστησεν.

Οὕτω καὶ τῶν ἀνθρώπων οἱ φύσει πονηροί, κἂν φύσιν
ἀλλάξωσι, τὸν γοῦν τρόπον οὐ μεταβάλλονται.

---

5   ἑαυτὸν 'his own (house)'
      Καθημένων...αὐτῶν gen. abs.
      Καθημένων gen. pl. perf. mid. (dep.) part. < κάθημαι
12   φύσει...φύσιν note word play with respect to the two meanings of φύσις
12-13 κἂν...ἀλλάξωσι...μεταβάλλονται pres. general condit.
      κἂν = καὶ + ἄν (= ἐάν [= εἰ + ἄν]) 'even if' (+ subju.)

Weasel in Ancient Greece

Some weasels took up residence in Greek houses, but they were most likely not kept as pets. In fact, when they are mentioned, it is alongside other vermin such as house mice. In addition, they were known to steal food. In describing the marten, a larger member of the mustelid family, Aristotle, *History of Animals* 8(9).6, says that it has τοῦ ἤθους τὴν κακουργίαν ὅμοιον γαλῆ ("a malicious character similar to that of the weasel").

Perhaps the most famous depiction of the weasel in Ancient Greek literature is from Semonides's notoriously misogynistic poem Fr. 7 (c. 625 BCE), in which he equates various types of women to different creatures and elements: "Another is from the weasel, a wretched, miserable sort. / She has nothing beautiful or charming / about her, nothing delightful or lovely. / She is mad for bed and lovemaking, / but any man who lies with her she sickens with disgust. / Her thieving does great harm to her neighbors, / and she often eats up offerings left unburned." (lines 50-56, trans. Andrew Miller)

ἀγανακτέω, be angry; + κατά τινος, 'be
   angry at/with someone or something'
ἀλλάσσω/ἀλλάττω, change, alter
ἄνθρωπος, ὁ, man, person
ἀπάγω, - άξω, -ήγαγον, lead away,
   bring back
ἀποκαθίστημι, -καταστήσω,
   -κατέστησα, reestablish, restore
ἀρχαῖος, -α, -ον, original, former
αὐτός, -ή, -ό, (adj.) -self, -selves;
   (pron. in gen., dat., acc.) him, her, it;
   them
Ἀφροδίτη, ἡ, Aphrodite; sexual love
βούλομαι, wish (+ inf.)
γαλέη/γαλῆ, -ῆς, ἡ, weasel, ferret
γι(γ)νώσκω, γνώσομαι, ἔγνων, learn
γοῦν (particle), οὖν ('then') + γε (putting
   emphasis on the word that precedes it,
   except when that word is an article; in
   the latter case, it emphasizes the word
   or words that follow); (restrictive
   particle w/ inferential force), at any rate
γυνή, -αικός, ἡ, woman, wife
διώκω, chase, pursue
ἑαυτοῦ, -ῆς, -οῦ (reflex. pron. in gen.,
   dat., acc.), himself, herself, itself;
   themselves
εἰ (conj.), if
ἐλεέω/ἐλεάω, take pity on, pity
ἐξανίστημι, ἐξαναστήσω,
   ἐξανεστην (2nd aor.), raise up;
   (2nd aor.) stand up from one's seat,
   rise from bed
ἐπιλανθάνω ἐπιλήσω/ἐπιλήσομαι,
   ἐπέλησα, escape notice; (mid./pass.)
   forget (+ gen.)
ἔραμαι, ἐρασθήσομαι, ἠράσθην,
   love, desire passionately, lust after
   (+ gen.); fall in love
εὐειδής, -ές, good looking, beautiful,
   w/ an attractive shape/figure

εὐπρεπής, -ές, good looking,
   attractive, handsome
εὔχομαι, εὔξομαι, ηὐξάμην, pray
θάλαμος, ὁ, inner room, bedroom
θεάομαι, see; gaze at, watch
θέλω/ἐθέλω, be willing (+ inf.)
θεός, ἡ, goddess
κάθημαι, be seated, sit
καθίημι, καθήσω, καθῆκα, send
   down
κατεσθίω, κατέδομαι, κατέφαγον,
   eat up, devour
κοίτη, ἡ, bed, esp. marriage bed; act
   of going to bed; sex
κόρη, ἡ, girl
μέσον, τό, the middle; ἐς τὸ μέσον,
   in their midst, between (them)
μεταβάλλω, change, alter
μεταμορφόω, transform
μετατυπόω, transform
μῦς, μυός, ὁ, mouse
νεάνισκος, ὁ, youth, young man
οἴκαδε (adv.), to home, homeward
ὅπως (conj.), so that, in order that
   (+ subju./opt.)
οὕτω/οὕτως (adv.), so, thus
πάθος, τό, what one has suffered or
   experienced; suffering, misfortune;
   passion; condition, state
πάλιν (adv.), again, once more
πάρειμι, be present, be at hand; τὰ
   παρόντα, present circumstances,
   present situation
πονηρός, -ά, -όν, wicked, bad
σῶμα, -ματος, τό, body
τρόπος, ὁ, habits, character, nature
φύσις, -εως, ἡ, exterior form,
   physical appearance; nature; character,
   natural disposition; φύσει, by nature
ὡς (sometimes prep. + acc.) = εἰς/ἐπί

32. Athena and the Weasel
(Chambry 76 [Variant 2] = Perry 50)

Γαλῆ ἠράσθη ποτὲ ἀνδρὸς εὐπρεποῦς καὶ τὴν Ἀθηνᾶν
ἐδυσώπει ταύτην μεταμεῖψαι εἰς γυναῖκα καὶ ἐρασθῆναι
αὐτῆς καὶ τὸν ἄνδρα ἐκεῖνον· ὃ δὴ καὶ ἔπραξεν ἡ θεά. Ἔτι δὲ
τοῦ γάμου ὄντος, μῦς διέδραμεν ἐν τῷ μέσῳ. Ἡ δὲ τὰ
5 νυμφικὰ ῥίψασα καὶ τῇ φύσει ἀκολουθήσασα τὸν μῦν
κατεδίωκεν.

Ὅτι, κἂν πρὸς βραχύ τις ἐν ὑποκρίσει μορφῶται καὶ
κρύπτηται, ἡ φύσις τοῦτον διὰ τῶν ἔργων ἐξελέγχει.

---

1   Ἀθηνᾶν among all versions of this tale in Greek and Latin literature, this is
the only one that has Athena in place of Aphrodite/Venus. Since Athena was
a virgin goddess, entreating her to help one in matters of the heart would be
like asking Ares to participate in peace negotiations or Zeus to serve as a
marriage counselor. This must, therefore, be a (somewhat heavy-handed)
humorous substitution on the part of the storyteller

2   ταύτην either modifies τὴν Ἀθηνᾶν (in which case it amplifies the previous
word – i.e., 'this powerful goddess' – and for which one then has to sc. 'her'
as dir. obj. of μεταμεῖψαι), or it is the dir. obj. of μεταμεῖψαι, w/ something
like the meaning of 'this (creature that she was)'
μεταμεῖψαι aor. act. inf. < μεταμείβω

2-3 ἐρασθῆναι...ἐκεῖνον not quite parallel w/ the preceding acc. and inf.
clause dependent on ἐδυσώπει: lit., 'she entreats Athena (, this [great
goddess]'?) to change her into a woman and (she entreats her) also that that
man love/passionately desire her,' i.e., that the goddess make it so that that
man love her

4   Ἔτι δὲ τοῦ γάμου ὄντος gen. abs., i.e., w/ the wedding feast still in
progress

7   Ὅτι = Ὁ μῦθος/λόγος δηλοῖ ὅτι
κἂν...μορφῶται καὶ κρύπτηται...ἐξελέγχει pres. general condition
κἂν = καὶ + ἂν (= ἐὰν [εἰ + ἂν]), 'even if' (+ subju.)
πρὸς βραχύ 'for a short time,' 'briefly'

ἀκολουθέω, follow, be guided by, obey (+ dat.); follow (rarely + acc.)

ἀνήρ, ἀνδρός, ὁ, man, husband

Ἀθηνᾶ, ἡ, Athena

βραχύς, -εῖα, -ύ, short, brief

γαλέη/γαλῆ, -ῆς, ἡ, weasel, ferret

γάμος, ὁ, wedding, wedding feast

γυνή, -αικός, ἡ, woman, wife

δή (particle), now, in truth, indeed

διά (prep. + gen.), through, by

διατρέχω, διέδραμον (aor.), run across or about

δυσωπέω, entreat X (acc.) to do Y (inf.)

ἐκεῖνος, ἐκείνη, ἐκεῖνο, that; (pl.) those

ἐξελέγχω, confute, refute; put to the test or proof

ἔραμαι, ἐρασθήσομαι, ἠράσθην, love, desire passionately, lust after (+ gen.); fall in love

ἔργον, τό, deed, action

ἔτι (adv.), still

εὐπρεπής, -ές, good looking, attractive, handsome

θεά, ἡ, goddess

καταδιώκω, follow hard upon, pursue, closely; search for

κρύπτω, hide, conceal

μέσον, τό, the middle; ἐν τῷ μέσῳ, in their midst, in between (them)

μεταμείβω, change, transform

μορφόω, give form; (pass.) take on a form

μῦς, μυός, ὁ, mouse

νυμφικά, τά, lit., nuptial things (e.g., dress, demeanor, etc.); conjugal relations; things that made her a girl

ὅς, ἥ, ὅ (rel. pron.), who, whose, whom, which, that

ὅτι (conj.), that

οὗτος, αὕτη, τοῦτο, this; (pl.) these

ποτε (adv.), at some time, at one time, once (upon a time)

πράττω, do

ῥίπτω, throw, hurl

τις, τι, (gen. τινος) (indef. pron.) someone; something; anyone; anything

ὑπόκρισις, -εως, ἡ, playing a part, hypocrisy, pretense, insincerity, outward show

φύσις, φύσεως, ἡ, origin; nature; character; natural disposition

33. Aphrodite and the Weasel
(Babrius 32 = Perry 50)

Γαλῆ ποτ᾽ ἀνδρὸς εὐπρεποῦς ἐρασθείσῃ

δίδωσι σεμνὴ Κύπρις, ἡ πόθων μήτηρ,

μορφὴν ἀμεῖψαι καὶ λαβεῖν γυναικείην,

καλῆς γυναικός, ἧς τίς οὐκ ἔχειν ἦρα;

5   ἰδὼν δ᾽ ἐκεῖνος - ἐν μέρει γὰρ ἡλώκει -

γαμεῖν ἔμελλεν. ἡρμένου δὲ τοῦ δείπνου

παρέδραμεν μῦς· τὸν δὲ τῆς βαθυστρώτου

καταβᾶσα κοίτης ἐπεδίωκεν ἡ νύμφη.

γάμου δὲ δαιτὴ ᾽λέλυτο, καὶ καλῶς παίξας

10   Ἔρως ἀπῆλθε· τῇ φύσει γὰρ ἡττήθη.

1-4 Γαλῆ...γυναικός = ποτ᾽ σεμνὴ Κύπρις, ἡ πόθων μήτηρ, δίδωσι γαλῆ, ἐρασθείσῃ εὐπρεποῦς ἀνδρός, ἀμεῖψαι μορφὴν καὶ λαβεῖν (μορφὴν) γυναικείην, (μορφὴν) καλῆς γυναικός

2 ἡ πόθων μήτηρ or ἡ Πόθων μήτηρ (w/ personification; cf. Pausanias 1.43.6)

3 Note chiasmus: μορφὴν (A) ἀμεῖψαι (B) καὶ (C) λαβεῖν (B) γυναικείην (A)

4 ἧς τίς οὐκ ἔχειν ἦρα the rel. cl. is the third modifier of μορφὴν after the adj. γυναικείην and the gen. noun phrase καλῆς γυναικός. Each descriptor provides additional details that increasingly amplify the transformed weasel's attractiveness: 'of a woman,' 'of a beautiful woman,' 'of a (woman of such beauty that there was no one) who was not desiring to possess her/have her as wife'
ἧς grammatically, the rel. pron. should be acc., not gen., since it is the dir. obj. of ἔχειν. But often in Gk. (and occasionally in English) it retains the case of its antecedent (Smyth § 2522)
ἡλώκει 3rd sing. pluperf. act. indic. < ἁλίσκομαι; sc. 'by love/desire'

5 ἰδὼν masc. nom. sing. aor. act. part. < ὁράω/ὁρῶ

6 ἡρμένου δὲ τοῦ δείπνου gen. abs.
ἡρμένου gen. sing. perf. pass. part. < ἀείρω/αἴρω

7 τὸν = αὐτὸν

9 ᾽λέλυτο = ἐλέλυτο 3rd sing. pluperf. (w/ imperf. force) mid./pass. indic. < λύω

10 ἡττήθη 3rd sing. aor. pass. (dep.) indic. < ἡσσάομαι/ἡττάομαι

ἀείρω/αἴρω, take away, remove; clear away (dinner)

ἀλίσκομαι, be taken, caught, or seized

ἀμείβω, change, alter

ἀνήρ, ἀνδρός, ὁ, man, husband

ἀπέρχομαι, ἀπελεύσομαι, ἀπῆλθον, go away, depart

βαθύστρωτος, -η, -ον, spread w/ thick covers

γαλέη/γαλῆ, -ῆς, ἡ, weasel, ferret

γαμέω, marry

γάμος, ὁ, wedding, wedding feast

γυναικεῖος, -η, -ον, of or belonging to women/a woman, feminine

γυνή, -αικός, ἡ, woman, wife

δαίτη, ἡ, feast, banquet

δεῖπνον, τό, dinner

δίδωμι, δώσω, ἔδωκα, allow/grant X (dat.) to do Y (inf.)

ἐκεῖνος, ἐκείνη, ἐκεῖνο, that; (pl.) those

ἐπιδιώκω, chase after, pursue

ἔραμαι, ἐρασθήσομαι, ἠράσθην, love, desire passionately, lust after (+ gen.)

ἐράω, love, be in love w/ (+ gen.); desire to (+ inf.)

Ἔρως, -ωτος, ὁ, Eros, god of love

εὐπρεπής, -ές, good looking, attractive, handsome

ἔχω, have, possess; have as wife

ἡσσάομαι/ἡττάομαι (Attic), be less than, inferior to; be defeated, beaten, or overcome by (+ dat.)

καλός, -ή, -όν, beautiful

καλῶς (adv.), beautifully, finely (sometimes ironically)

καταβαίνω, καταβήσομαι, κατέβην, go or come down from (+ gen.)

κοίτη, ἡ, bed, esp. marriage bed; act of going to bed; sex

Κύπρις, -ιδος, ἡ, Kypris/Cypris (lit., the Cyprian woman), a name of Aphrodite derived from the island of Cyprus

λαμβάνω, λήψομαι, ἔλαβον, take

λύω, dissolve, break up; put an end to

μέλλω, intend to (+ fut. inf.)

μέρος, -εος, τό, one's turn; ἐν μέρει, in turn

μήτηρ, μητρός, ἡ, mother

μορφή, ἡ, form, shape, figure, appearance

μῦς, μυός, ὁ, mouse

νύμφη, ἡ, bride

ὁράω/ὁρῶ, ὄψομαι, εἶδον, see

ὅς, ἥ, ὅ (rel. pron.), who, whose, whom, which, that

παίζω, παίξομαι, ἔπαιξα, play, play a game, joke

παρατρέχω, -δραμοῦμαι, παρέδραμον, run by or past

πόθος, ὁ, longing, yearning, desire

ποτε (adv.), at some time, at one time, once (upon a time)

σεμνός, -ή, -όν, revered, holy, august; proud, haughty

τίς, τί (gen. τίνος; interrog. pron. and adj.), who? which? what?

φύσις, φύσεως, ἡ, origin; nature; character; natural disposition

L'Estrange (1692)

A *YOUNG Fellow* that was passionately in Love with a *Cat* made it his humble Suit to *Venus* to turn *Puss* into a *Woman*. The Transformation was wrought in the twinkling of an Eye, and out she comes, a very bucksome Lass. The doating Sot took her home to his Bed; and bad fair for a Litter of Kittens by her that Night: But as the loving Couple lay snugging together, a Toy took *Venus* in the Head, to try if the *Cat* had chang'd her Manners with her Shape; and so for Experiment, turn'd a *Mouse* loose into the Chamber. The *Cat*, upon this Temptation, started out of the Bed, and without any regard to the Marriage-Joys, made a leap at the *Mouse*, which *Venus* took for so high an Affront, that she turn'd the Madam into a *Puss* again.

THE MORAL. *The extravagant Transports of Love, and the wonderful Force of Nature, are unaccountable; the one carries us out of our selves, and the other brings us back again.*

REFLECTION. This is to lay before us the Charms and Extravagances of a blind Love. It covers all Imperfections, and considers neither Quality, nor Merit. How many noble Whores has it made, and how many imperial Slaves! And let the Defects be never so gross, it either palliates, or excuses them. The *Woman*'s leaping at the *Mouse*, tells us also how impossible it is to make Nature change her biass, and that *if we shut her out at the Door, she'll come in at the Window.*

Here's the Image of a wild and fantastical Love, under the Cover of as extravagant a Fable, and it is all but fancy at last too; for Men do not see, or taste, or find the Thing they love, but they create it. They fashion an Idol, in what figure or shape they please; set it up, worship it, dote upon it, pursue it, and, in fine, run mad for't. How many Passions have we seen in the World, ridiculous enough to answer all the Follies of this Imagination! It was much for *Venus* to turn the *Cat* into a *Woman*, and for that Cully again to take that *Cat* for a *Woman:* What is it less now, for a Fop to form an *Idea* of a *Woman* he dies for, every jot as unlike that *Woman*, as the *Cat* is to the *Mistress*? Let this suffice for the Impostures, and Illusions of that Passion.

We are further given to understand that no Counterfeit is so steady and so equally drawn, but Nature by Starts will shew herself thorough it; for *Puss*, even when she's a *Madam*, will be a *Mouser* still. 'Tis the same Thing with a Hypocrite, which is only a Devil dress'd up with a Ray about him, and transform'd into an Angel of Light. Take him in the very Raptures of his Devotion, and do but throw a parcel of *Church-Lands* in his Way, he shall leap at the Sacrilege from the very Throne of his Glory, as *Puss* did at the *Mouse*; and pick your Pocket, as a *French* poet says of a *Jesuit*, in the middle of his *Pater-Noster*.

Linton (1887)

"Might his Cat be a woman", he said:
Venus changed her: the couple were wed:
But a mouse in her sight
Metamorphosed her quite,
And, for a bride, a cat found he instead.

NATURE WILL OUT

Jacobs (1894)

The gods were once disputing whether it was possible for a living being to change its nature. Jupiter said "Yes," but Venus said "No." So, to try the question, Jupiter turned a Cat into a Maiden, and gave her to a young man for a wife. The wedding was duly performed and the young couple sat down to the wedding-feast. "See," said Jupiter, to Venus, "how becomingly she behaves. Who could tell that yesterday she was but a Cat? Surely her nature is changed?"

"Wait a minute," replied Venus, and let loose a mouse into the room. No sooner did the bride see this than she jumped up from her seat and tried to pounce upon the mouse. "Ah, you see," said Venus, "nature will out."

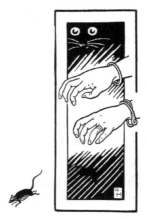

Richard Heighway (1894)

119

La Fontaine (1668)
(trans. Hill [2008])

A man adored his cat to an insane degree:
How delicate, how darling, how delightful, she!
Her mew made such a melting music in his ears
That finally, by prayers and tears,
By sorcery, spells and magic charms
He wheedled Fate to bend its laws
And change a cat with fur and claws
Into a woman with legs and arms –
Whom then, Sir Fool personified,
That very day he made his bride,
For love had driven him as mad
As, earlier, affection had.
No beauty celebrated for
The amorous career she led
Ever pleased a lover more
Than this new bride her groom, new wed.
He sweet-talked her, she called him honey,
And so the two – hey, nonny, nonny!
He found in her no trace of cat,
Certain, as his delusion grew,
She was pure woman, through and through.
But when one night soon after that

Some mice made noises gnawing underneath their bed
Then instantly the wife assumed
A cattish crouch: the mice all fled.
The mice returned. Now she resumed
Her feline posture, as before,
And this time pounced upon her prey,
For since she'd metamorphosed they
Were less inclined to fear her anymore –
While they to her proved bait, whose source
Of power over her was nature's shaping force
That mocks at any change once time enough has passed.
Emptied, the vessel smells; once made, the crease will last,

The wheel stays in its rutted track,
What's done grows past undoing, nothing will change it back.

Strike nature with your pitchforks, take your whips to it,
You won't reform it, not one bit.
Advance together, sticks in hand,
It won't obey though you command.
Slam your door in its face when nature comes to knock –
And it will climb through windows your forgot to lock.

Alexander Calder (1931)

121

34. Zeus and Man
(Chambry 57/57 = Perry 108)

Λέγουσι πρῶτον τὰ ζῷα πλασθῆναι καὶ χαρισθῆναι
αὐτοῖς παρὰ θεοῦ, τῷ μὲν ἀλκήν, τῷ δὲ τάχος, τῷ δὲ
πτερά, τὸν δὲ ἄνθρωπον γυμνὸν ἑστῶτα εἰπεῖν· "Ἐμὲ
μόνον κατέλιπες ἔρημον χάριτος." τὸν δὲ Δία εἰπεῖν·
5   "Ἀνεπαίσθητος εἶ τῆς δωρεᾶς, καίτοι τοῦ μεγίστου
τετυχηκώς· λόγον γὰρ ἔχεις λαβών, ὃς παρὰ θεοῖς δύναται
καὶ παρὰ ἀνθρώποις, τῶν δυνατῶν δυνατώτερος καὶ τῶν
ταχίστων ταχύτερος." Καὶ τότε ἐπιγνοὺς τὸ δῶρον ὁ
ἄνθρωπος προσκυνήσας καὶ εὐχαριστήσας ᾤχετο.

10   Ὅτι, ἐκ θεοῦ λόγῳ τιμηθέντων πάντων ἀνεπαισθήτως
ἔχουσί τινες τῆς τοιαύτης τιμῆς καὶ μᾶλλον ζηλοῦσι τὰ
ἀναίσθητα καὶ ἄλογα ζῷα.

---

1   **Λέγουσι** sets up indir. disc. w/ acc. + inf. in lines 1, 3, and 5
πλασθῆναι aor. pass. inf. < πλάσσω
χαρισθῆναι aor. pass. inf. < χαρίζω/χαρίζομαι; sc. δῶρα as acc. subj. of
the inf.

2   **θεοῦ** when unnamed, usually refers to Zeus, as l. 4 confirms
τῷ μὲν..., τῷ δὲ... to one..., to another..., etc. (Smyth § 1107).

3   **ἑστῶτα** masc. acc. sing. perf. act. part. < ἵστημι

5   **τοῦ μεγίστου** one expects fem., in agreement w/ τῆς δωρεᾶς. Either sc.
δώρου or translate as neut.

6   **τετυχηκώς** masc. nom. sing. perf. act. part. < τυγχάνω
λόγον...ἔχεις λαβὼν ἔχω + aor. part. = auxiliary vb. giving a perf. sense,
i.e., 'you have taken λόγος (and are now in possession of it)'

7-8 **τῶν δυνατῶν...τῶν ταχίστων** gens. of comparison (Smyth § 1068,
1069). Note that in Greek the comp. adj. can *follow* a gen. of comparison

10 **Ὅτι** = ὁ μῦθος δηλοῖ ὅτι
λόγῳ instrumental dat. (Smyth § 1503)
τιμηθέντων πάντων gen. abs. w/ concessive force, i.e., although...
τιμηθέντων gen. pl. aor. pass. part. < τιμάω

10-11 **ἀνεπαισθήτως ἔχουσί τινες** = ἀνεπαίσθητοι εἰσί τινες (cf. l. 5). Gk.
ἔχω + adv. = English εἰμί + adj. (Smyth § 1438)

ἀλκή, ἡ, strength

ἄλογος, -ον, w/out or lacking in λόγος;
  unreasoning; τὰ ἄλογα, brute beasts,
  animals

ἀναίσθητος, -ον, w/out or lacking in
  sense

ἀνεπαίσθητος, -ον, not perceiving
  or noticing X (gen.)

ἀνεπαισθήτως (adv.), in a manner not
  perceiving or noticing X (gen.)

ἄνθρωπος, ὁ, man, person, human being

αὐτός, -ή, -ό, (pron. in gen., dat., acc.)
  him, her, it; them

γυμνός, -ή, -όν, naked

δηλόω, show, reveal

δύναμαι, be powerful, has power

δυνατός, -ή, -όν, strong, powerful

δυνατώτερος, -η, -ον, stronger,
  more powerful

δωρεά, ἡ, gift

δῶρον, τό, gift

ἐγώ, ἐμοῦ, ἐμοί, ἐμέ, I, me

ἐκ (prep. + gen. w/ pass. voice), by

ἐπιγι(γ)νώσκω, ἐπιγνώσομαι,
  ἐπέγνων, recognize

ἔρημος, -ον, w/out, lacking (+ gen.)

εὐχαριστέω, offer thanks, be thankful

Ζεύς, Διός, Διΐ, Δία, ὁ, Zeus

ζηλόω, be jealous of, envy

ζῷον/ζῶον, τό, animal, creature

θεός, ὁ, god

ἵστημι, make stand; (2nd aor.; perf.) stand

καίτοι/καί τοι (part.), although; and
  indeed, and what is more

καταλείπω, καταλείψω,
  κατέλιπον, leave

λαμβάνω, λήψομαι, ἔλαβον, take,
  seize

λέγω, λέξω/ἐρῶ, εἶπον, say

λόγος, ὁ, speech, language; power of
  speech; thinking, reasoning, reflection,
  deliberation

μᾶλλον (adv.), rather, instead

μέγιστος, -η, -ον, greatest

μονός, -ή, -όν, alone, only

μῦθος, ὁ, story, fable, tale

οἴχομαι, ᾠχόμην (imperf.), be gone

ὅς, ἥ, ὅ (rel. pron.), who, whose,
  whom, which, that

ὅτι (conj.), that

παρά (prep. + gen.), by; from; (+ dat.)
  with, among

πᾶς, πᾶσα, πᾶν, all, every

πλάσσω, form; (pass.) be molded,
  made

προσκυνέω, fall down and worship,
  prostrate oneself before

πρῶτον (adv.), first, in the beginning

πτερόν, τό, wing

τάχιστος, -η, -ον, swiftest, quickest

τάχος, -εος, τό, swiftness, speed

ταχύτερος, -η, -ον, swifter, quicker

τιμάω, honor

τιμή, ἡ, honor

τις, τι, (gen. τινος), (indef. pron.)
  someone, a certain person; something

τοιοῦτος, -αύτη, -οῦτο, such as
  this; (frequently w/ implication based
  on context) so good/bad/etc. ...as this

τότε (adv.), then, at that time

τυγχάνω, get, obtain (+ gen.); (perf.)
  be in possession of, have (+ gen.)

χαρίζω/χαρίζομαι, give; (pass.)
  (of a thing) to be given or bestowed

χάρις, χάριτος, ἡ, gift

λόγος/ἄλογος

Gibbs (237-8) notes that: "The gift given to mankind is called *logos* in Greek, which refers both to speech and to rational thought. The Greeks regularly referred to animals as *aloga*, or lacking in *logos*. This Greek phrase thus has a double meaning much like the English expression 'dumb animals,' which is used to indicate animals who are both speechless and (supposedly) stupid. For a different account of the creation, see Plato, *Protagoras* 320C ff., where the defenceless human race is armed by Prometheus with fire."

Other Ancient Greek and Latin Intermediate Readers by the Author

Ancient Greek

The Infancy Gospel of Thomas

[*The Infancy Gospel of Thomas* (c. 150 CE) is an excellent text for students who have completed the first year of college-level Ancient Greek. Its length is short, its syntax is generally straightforward, and its narrative is inherently interesting, for it is the only account from the period of early Christianity that tells of the childhood of Jesus. This student edition includes grammatical, syntactical, literary, historical, and cultural notes. Complete vocabulary is provided for each section of the text, with special attention paid to the differences between Koine Greek and Classical Greek meanings and usage. Since *The Infancy Gospel of Thomas* possesses an unusually rich textual history, this edition also includes a selection of the most interesting variant readings.]

Lucian, *On the Death of Peregrinus*

[Lucian's *On the Death of Peregrinus* is an excellent text for students who have completed the first year of college-level Ancient Greek or its equivalent. Its length is relatively short, its syntax is generally straightforward, and its narrative is inherently interesting, for it recounts the life of a man who was so determined to establish a new religious cult to himself that he committed suicide at the Olympic Games in 165 CE by self-immolation. Lucian, an eyewitness to this event, depicts Peregrinus as a glory-obsessed impostor who began his career as an adulterer, pederast, and parricide before becoming a leader of the Christian Church, a Cynic philosopher, and an aspiring "divine guardian of the night." Also of interest to readers today is that Lucian's text contains some of the earliest and most interesting comments made by a member of the Greco-Roman educated elite concerning Jesus and the Christians of the 2nd century CE. This edition includes detailed grammatical, syntactical, literary, historical, and cultural notes. Complete vocabulary is provided for each section of the text, with a glossary of all words at the end.]

Lucian, *True Stories*

[Lucian's *True Stories* is an excellent text for students who have completed the first year of college-level Ancient Greek or its equivalent. Its length is relatively modest, its syntax is generally straightforward, and its narrative – a sophisticated satire that blends elements of fantasy and science fiction – is both engaging and thought-provoking. This edition includes extensive grammatical, syntactical, rhetorical, literary, historical, biographical, and cultural notes. Complete vocabulary is provided for each section of the text, with special attention paid to Lucian's comic verbal coinages. Since Lucian's *True Stories* abounds with references to and appropriations from nine centuries of Ancient Greek literature, this edition also includes a generous selection of comparative passages (including the entirety of Iambulus' "Journey to the Islands of the Sun") to assist the student in appreciating still more this cunningly crafted and densely allusive work.]

Xenophon of Ephesus, *An Ephesian Tale*

[Xenophon of Ephesus's "pulp-fiction" novel, *An Ephesian Tale*, is an excellent text for students who have completed the first year of college-level Ancient Greek or its equivalent. Its length is quite short, its syntax is straightforward, and its narrative – an adventure romance between two young ill-starred lovers (Habrocomes and Anthia) – is one of the most action-packed and enjoyable in all of Ancient Greek literature. This edition includes brief grammatical, syntactical, rhetorical, and cultural notes. Complete vocabulary is provided for each section of the text.]

Ancient Greek Cyclops Tales (Homer, Euripides, Theocritus, Callimachus, and Lucian)

[forthcoming – 2017]

Ancient Greek Lyric Poetry (a selection)

[forthcoming – 2018]

Latin

A Medieval Latin Miscellany (with Art Robson)

[This Medieval Latin reader is aimed at intermediate undergraduate/ advanced high school Latin students. The texts included in this collection cover religious biography (excerpts from Jerome's *Life of Hilarion*), tall-tales (*Asinarius* and *Rapularius*), heroic journey (*Alexander the Great Meets Thalestris, Queen of the Amazons* and Letaldus of Micy's *The Fisherman Swallowed by a Whale*), fables (Odo of Cheriton) and jokes (Poggio Bracciolini). Introductions to each text, as well as assistance with vocabulary, grammar, and syntax are provided.]

Three Medieval Latin Liturgical Dramas

[This edition makes available to intermediate Latin students three dramatic works of Medieval Latin literature. The earliest of these, the eleventh-century *Tres Clerici* ("The Three Students"), recounts one of the miracles of that most popular of medieval saints, Nicholas. This drama's economical construction and

126

refined use of a simple metrical unit exemplify how a playwright can convey much in few words. The other two plays included in this collection are the outstanding examples of Latin liturgical drama composed in the twelfth century. The *Danielis Ludus* ("The Play of Daniel"), written in the cathedral school of Beauvais, adapts material from the Bible to relate the meaning of a story from the ancient past – the Hebrew prophet Daniel's interactions with two foreign rulers, Belshazzar and Darius – to contemporary issues. This play's rhetorical sophistication, metrical variety, and musical invention are unsurpassed in the dramatic works from this period. Hildegard of Bingen's *Ordo Virtutum* ("The Play of the Virtues") has the distinction of being the only play in this group whose author is not anonymous. Hildegard left behind more than just a name, however, for her impressive literary, scientific, theological, and musical oeuvre rivals those of her more traditionally educated male peers in quality and surpasses them in diversity. In addition, Hildegard's female-centered play, whose verses are rich with symbolism, fuses together liturgical drama and theological allegory in an innovative manner that anticipates the new genre of morality plays written in the vernacular languages two centuries later. This edition provides significant assistance with vocabulary, grammar, and syntax, with special attention paid to Medieval Latin forms. There are also extensive literary and historical notes.]

Gesta Francorum: An Eyewitness Account of the First Crusade

[forthcoming - 2018]

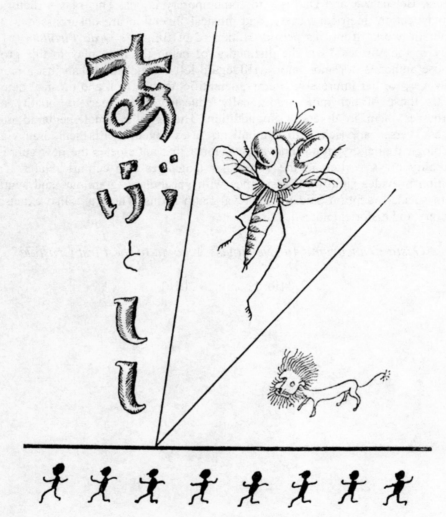

Takeo Takei (1925)

CPSIA information can be obtained
at www.ICGtesting.com
Printed in the USA
LVHW061546020723
751375LV00007B/813